A Flame for Justice

Two brothers struggled to live among the intense pressures of Soweto township. Each chose a different way to survive. One joined the military wing of the African National Congress and served a prison sentence.

This is the true story of the second brother, Caesar Molebatsi. Maimed for life by a white man, he had more reason than most to hate. Yet he learned to forgive, and developed a passionate concern for the youth of Soweto.

Caesar Molebatsi is executive director of Youth Alive Ministries and a founding member of Ebenezer Evangelical Church. A frequent speaker on missions and social-justice issues, he and his family live in Soweto, South Africa.

David Virtue, born in New Zealand, is a freelance writer who previously worked as a journalist in New Zealand and Canada and later wrote for the American Bible Society, American Leprosy Missions and World Vision International. He and his family live in West Chester, Pennsylvania.

A Flame for Justice

Caesar Molebatsi

with David Virtue

A LION PAPERBACK
Oxford · Batavia · Sydney

Published by
Lion Publishing plc
Sandy Lane West, Oxford, England
ISBN 0 7459 1482 9
Lion Publishing Corporation
1705 Hubbard Avenue, Batavia, Illinois 60510, USA
ISBN 0 7459 1482 9
Albatross Books Pty Ltd
P.O. Box 320, Sutherland, NSW 2232, Australia
ISBN 0 7324 0284 0

First edition 1991

British Library Cataloguing in Publication Data
Molebatsi, Caesar
  A flame for justice.
  I. Title II. Virtue, David
  305.800968
  ISBN 0 7459 1482 9

Library of Congress Cataloging-in-Publication Data
(Applied for)

Printed and bound in Great Britain by
Cox & Wyman Ltd, Reading

Preface

I am indebted to many for this book.

Caesar gave of his time so unstintingly amidst the heavy demands and the long hours he labors serving his Lord and his brothers and sisters in Soweto.

His wife, Chumi, assumed more than her usual heavy load to allow Caesar the days and nights necessary to write this book and be away from their four children. She has been a singular source of strength to him throughout his ministry.

Murray Watts, British playwright and director, contributed to the manuscript in its initial form.

Sam and Nunu Molebatsi, Caesar's brother and sister-in-law, graciously allowed me to write in the comfort and safety of their home in Dobsonville, Soweto, on my first trip to South Africa.

Cliff and Eileen Buckwalter took me into their home in Eldorado Park, a so-called coloured area near Soweto, so I could finish the manuscript in peace and quiet during my second trip to South Africa.

And, not least, I am indebted to my wife, Mary, who took over all my responsibilities, freeing me to travel twice to South Africa and to write without encumbrances.

Above all, this book is dedicated to my black brothers and sisters of Ebenezer Evangelical Church and to the thousands of men, women and children of Soweto who live under the iron fist of institutionalized racism—for that is what apartheid is—and who must daily suffer the indignities of that system. I salute you.

My prayer is that, through the work of the church, justice, mercy and righteousness will prevail and that rivers of living water will flow, bringing new economic and political structures, educational opportunities and hope to a new generation of black brothers and sisters.

David W. Virtue
West Chester, Pennsylvania

Contents

Introduction

It is Christmas 1990 as I watch with a saddened and heavy heart the violence that racks Soweto night after night. It is a nightmare of a thousand deaths, unnecessary deaths. Our communities are stunned and paralyzed with fear. Black-on-black violence has spread from the province of Natal to the townships of Johannesburg where I live.

In truth, violence has touched every corner of our nation. No one can escape its powerful grip. All of us—men, women, children, black, white, rich and poor—have come face to face with the harsh reality of violence. The carnage appears indiscriminately on train-station platforms, on bus and taxi ranks, even in homes. No place is safe. No end is in sight. Sadly we have come to expect this carnage. Most accept it passively. It is almost a way of life.

There are more questions than there are answers. With every step forward there seem to be two steps back. As the path to a new South Africa unfolds, more doubts arise on both sides of the political spectrum about what sort of future it will be, what sort of country will emerge from the chaos.

As I look out at South Africa from my corner of strife-torn Soweto, I ask myself this question: "Is there anything in our collective religious faith that can bring respite and hope to this beleagured nation?" It is ironic that this nation claims to be God-fearing and Christian. I ask myself, as a Christian leader, what the role of the church should be in the midst of all this uncertainty and fear. Many of us who have been involved in the struggle for justice see the church seeming to beat a hasty retreat in the face of the struggle. We are told that the church must get out of the business of politics.

The measures that President F. W. de Klerk took last February, including the release of Nelson Mandela and the sanction of the African National Congress along with thirty-three other organizations, provided hope for a different future for the people of South Africa. These measures appeared to be the prelude to fundamental change. But despite these developments, the vast majority of blacks have as yet seen no change in the dismal quality of their lives. Talks are being sabotaged by those whose personal or political interests are threatened by the changes. Clearly, an equitable settlement will not be reached by groups who are motivated by racist attitudes on the one hand and by mistrust on the other. And as one fragile peace pact after another is broken, it seems there will be no end to the bloodshed.

I know that the only way forward is through reconciliation between the races. This will take a major commitment on the part of all South Africans, especially those who call themselves Christians. But it is the only chance we have.

Caesar Molebatsi
Soweto, South Africa

1

The Accident

It was December 24—a beautiful afternoon like many in Johannesburg during the Christmas season. I was on my bicycle rounding the curve of a road near my home when, without warning, a car coming from behind struck me and hurled me from my bike.

I had been so intently focusing on a car coming toward me that I was only vaguely aware of the car behind trying to pass me on the narrow road. Instead of braking or slowing down when he saw the oncoming car, the driver behind continued at the same high speed. When he realized that he couldn't overtake me in time, he had to make a quick decision: either slow down to let me get ahead and then move back into the driving lane, thereby risking a collision with the oncoming car; or else swerve immediately back into the driving lane, thereby risking the life of a black boy on a bike. He jerked the wheel in my direction.

The impact sent me reeling across the brittle tarmac surface of the road. In a split second I was a tangle of shattered bones with bicycle parts protruding from different parts of my body. I lay in the road bleeding profusely; my right kneecap was completely crushed. My leg was broken above and below the knee. The bicycle handlebars had sliced through my right side, spilling part of my innards onto the road. My head throbbed.

For what seemed like hours, I lay helplessly entangled in the bicycle, floating in and out of consciousness until a police van finally arrived. The driver, a white man, picked me off the road and dumped me unceremoniously into the back of his van, like I was a sack of potatoes. Then he took off at high speed to a nearby clinic in Swartruggens. During the ride I lapsed into unconsciousness.

At the clinic the staff discovered that, in addition to my leg damage, I had sustained severe injuries to the back of my head from my impact with the road. After a brief examination, the nurses realized how serious my injuries were and how little they could do with the resources they had. They patched me up as best they could, outfitted me with an intravenous drip and put me back into the police van for a thirty-five-mile journey to Rustenburg Hospital.

I will never know how I survived that journey. I lost blood throughout the trip. When I regained consciousness during the ride, the pain was so intense that I cried out in agony. I wanted desperately to slip back into unconsciousness in order to avoid the pain, but I couldn't. The driver ignored my cries. I later learned that he became angry and abusive when he discovered that his van was covered in kaffir blood.

At the hospital I was rushed into the operating room. My last thoughts before slipping back into unconsciousness were, "I'm going to die. Is this the way it's supposed to end?" When I awoke from the operation several hours later, surrounded by white walls, piped-in music and religious wall hangings, I thought I actually had died and gone to heaven.

I had never thought much about religion up to that point in my life. My family were no longer great churchgoers. For many years, my father had been a staunch Anglican church member and superintendent at Sunday school. So we children attended church when we were young. But because of the hypocrisy my father encountered over racial issues, he abandoned the church completely; and we soon followed his example. As a teenager, I simply hadn't seen the need for religion and couldn't be bothered to think about it.

But the awful experience of that accident shook me up pretty badly. As I lay on the bed feeling stiff and sore, my head in bandages, I began to think seriously about life and religion for the first time. Why did this accident happen? What if I had died? If there was a God, what did he have to do with all this?

As I struggled with those questions and with the pain of my injuries, a white missionary from the German Lutheran church came into my hospital room. It was Christmas morning, and he came to offer me a gift. Without even introducing himself, he came up to my bed and asked me to accept the Bible he brought. He also wanted to chat with me for a bit, but I wasn't in the mood. "Look," I said, "I don't want to talk—to you or to anybody." Without a word he turned and left. I later discovered the Bible by my bed, but I was too occupied by pain and self-pity to bother reading it.

In fact, I was so obsessed with grief and self-pity that I took little notice of anything else. Even the visits of my family brought little comfort.

After spending twenty days on my back, I took a turn for the worse. Gangrene had set in on my lower right leg. According to the doctors, this explained the pain in my thigh. I was given heavier doses of morphine, but no amount of pain killers could give me relief.

When the doctors tested the leg again there was no feeling around my knee. Nothing. Their attempts to patch the blood vessels on both sides of the knee had failed. The doctors decided to amputate my leg before the gangrene spread further.

My first inkling of what lay in store came when my mother described the seriousness of my situation and began apologizing for the doctors. She told me that I must be a man and accept the inevitability of the situation; she could not bring herself to tell me that the doctors were going to cut off my leg. While my mother talked, I could see the doctors hovering in the background.

Finally, one of the doctors moved closer to the bed. Standing next to my mother, he explained how they were going to amputate my leg. He tried to console me with assurances that many other people had lost their legs and this was not the end of my life or the end of the world. They had tried their best to save my leg, he said, but there was nothing more they could do.

When I was brought to the hospital on December 24, 1964, I was a wreck, but I had high hopes for recovery. On January 13, 1965, those hopes rapidly sank as I was wheeled into the operating room. I knew that they were going to cut off my right leg above the knee. One part of my body would go to the incinerator, and the rest of me would live. This awful realization frightened me enormously.

When I awoke after several hours in the operating room, I felt numb. I knew my leg was gone, but I could not accept that knowledge. Together the doctors and my family tried to help. They explained things like "phantom pain." They described new technologies now being used in prostheses. They assured me that the loss of a leg would not totally immobilize me. But my sense of loss was deep and would not go away.

Again my thoughts turned to religion. And for the first time in my life I experienced deep hatred and bitterness. I began to think that if there was a God, he was a most unloving and unkind God—not only to me personally, but also to my people.

What kind of a God would allow me, a black, already dispossessed in my own land, to be further victimized and brutalized by a single white man? What kind of God would allow me to lose a leg, thereby possibly depriving me of any future I might have in my own country? Blacks were little more than a source of manual labor for the white man in South Africa, and now I would cease to have even that usefulness.

As the days and weeks passed, my anger deepened and expanded beyond my personal tragedy. I asked myself what kind of God would allow an entire race of people—whose skin happened to be black—to be duped and cheated out of what was historically, culturally and geographically theirs by a small minority race—whose skin happened to be white.

Ironically, as my hate deepened, my body began to heal. If there is a relationship between hate and healing, I had never

14

heard of it. Perhaps my hatred fueled my will to live. Whatever it was, the pace of healing came swiftly, and the day came for me to be discharged from the hospital.

My father arrived to take me home, and I was pleased to see him. He had visited only three times during my four-month stay in the hospital. Those infrequent visits were very difficult for him because, deep down, he blamed himself for my accident. In the busyness of that Christmas Eve day, my father had asked me to go Christmas shopping alone on a bicycle instead of with him in the van. He had never forgiven himself for that request. He never spoke about the loss of my leg, but I knew he felt the pain of my loss very deeply.

I left the hospital that April morning in 1965 a bitter and angry young man, minus one leg and without a future that I could see. With my father at my side, I hobbled nervously into a bleak and uncertain world.

During my stay in the hospital, my father had attempted to put together a legal case against the man who had almost killed me. He felt a great injustice had been done me, and he sought justice.

Soon after we returned home, the police called on us. After four months, and because of my father's insistence, they had come to see us about the accident. The police claimed that they already had taken a statement from me at the hospital, but I didn't recall giving them one. Because of my mistrust of the police, I would not have believed them even if they had shown me a signed copy of the statement.

I learned that the driver had accused me of being drunk at the time of the accident. This accusation was a lie and a terrible blow to my self-respect. Whatever mistakes I may have made on the bicycle that day, one thing was certain: I was not drunk. I have never been drunk in my life. Despite my angry protests, however, the police believed the white man's story. When they finally left, I felt betrayed and enraged. I knew that the system, run and controlled by whites, would never give me justice.

The experiences surrounding the accident took a heavy toll on me. I felt too humiliated and defeated to return to school; I couldn't even bear to face my family. I needed to get away, to be alone with my thoughts.

I moved out of our home and stayed for eight months on a farm near Rustenburg, the town where I had been hospitalized. I was put up in a two-room frame house occupied by my father's cousin, whom we called "uncle," and his wife.

"Uncle" Dan was an educated man who lived on a pittance of a wage in order to teach rural black kids, many of whom walked thirty kilometers (eighteen miles), each day, to his makeshift schoolhouse. These were black children who otherwise would never have had the opportunity for an education. "Schools" such as his were provided by white farmers with some government subsidies, and they generally offered only the most minimal education for poor rural black children. Uncle Dan, however, treated his students as though they were his own children. He believed that if there was a way for blacks to improve their situation, it would be through education. And he was determined to do whatever he could to see that black young people got an education.

For the rest of 1965 I hid away on that farm. During this time, Uncle Dan and his wife literally kept me alive. They loved me and patiently accepted my mood swings. Their patience knew no bounds.

My daily schedule consisted of getting up in the morning, picking up a lot of books—mainly junk—and hobbling out into the big orchard to sit under a tree and read and think. For some strange reason, I still had the Bible I had been given in the hospital, and from time to time I would turn over its pages and read it. Most of the time, however, I just sat there feeling sorry for myself.

After eight months had passed, my father came to visit. He pointedly told me that I couldn't go on living like this and that I would have to return home with him. I put up little resistance, knowing he was right. Reluctantly I said goodbye to my uncle and his wife and returned to Soweto and to school.

Back at home, I coped with life by showing two different faces to the world. When I was out in public, I acted as though I had adjusted to life without a leg. I carried on as though nothing were wrong. I hid the pain from everyone, moving through each day as though it were business as usual.

When I was alone or with my family, however, I was a different person—an angry and despairing person. Uncontrollable fits of rage frequently erupted in me, and I would swing my crutch around my head and smash it to smithereens. My family never challenged the destruction. They knew I had not yet come to terms with my loss and that I would have to do this in my own way and time.

Occasionally I played soccer with neighborhood friends, swinging from crutch to crutch, vaulting around the field after the ball. When I was alone after the game, I became depressed. I wondered how people saw me. What did they think when they looked at me playing soccer with crutches? Was I a fascinating oddity perhaps, like a circus performer? Or did they interpret my efforts as a denial of the fact that I was a cripple?

On the surface I gave people the impression that I was strong and that nothing could touch me. Deep down I yearned for somebody to truly understand the inadequacies I felt because I was crippled and to help me express the feelings of bitterness and hatred I felt toward whites.

A year had passed and we had not heard a word from the police. My patience had run out, as had my father's. He took the initiative one winter day to go to the police station and ask if any action had been taken. My father still believed that the courts would give us justice. I had no such confidence, but I went along to see what would happen.

When we arrived, the commandant and the policeman who had investigated the accident were both there. They told me to wait outside the station while the investigating policeman and my father withdrew into the interview office.

Outside, I huddled against the wall of the police station

and tried to shield myself from the cold veldt winds. I ached to know what was going on inside, but I tried hard to be patient.

When my father emerged from the interview some forty minutes later, I saw tears in his eyes. Without a word he motioned that we were leaving. I had never before seen my father cry, and I was deeply moved. He remained silent as we walked home, and I had to plead with him to tell me what took place inside the police station.

When he finally regained his composure, my father explained; his words stabbed like an arrow into my soul. The policeman told him that we were like all blacks—always looking for a way to take money from whites without working for it. He also said that my father ought to be glad I hadn't died. In saying this, the policeman used the word "vrek"—an Afrikaans term used to describe the death of an animal. In essence, the policeman's response to my father's plea for justice was to call us lazy, greedy animals.

When my father had finished, I was burning with anger and hatred. God, how I hated that policeman! How I hated all whites! My only thoughts were for revenge. If the corrupt white man's system would not give me justice, then I would seek my own justice.

The year was 1966. I was a seventeen-year-old crippled black, living in a country dominated by corrupt whites. Together with my younger brother George, I plotted revenge. We made a pact to find the white man who had crippled me and burn his house to the ground. We were passionately committed to this act of vengeance. I didn't care if I got arrested, I didn't care what might happen to me. I was determined to have revenge, no matter what it cost.

2

The Seeds of Bitterness

Soweto lies fifteen miles southwest of Johannesburg. It is an ugly beast of a town borne out of the malignant policy of apartheid. Soweto became this beast as a result of two laws passed by the new apartheid government in 1948. The first was the Homeland Policy, which stated that blacks could never own land—even if it was land they had lived on for generations. This law gave the government the right to uproot and dispossess blacks.

The second law was the Group Areas Act, which dictated that the different races, such as coloured, white and Indian, had to live in ethnically prescribed areas. This law empowered the government to herd all blacks from across the 175-mile reef, where gold and diamonds were mined, into the new settlement of Soweto.

Soweto became—and still is—South Africa's biggest eyesore. It is a squalid shantytown created by the government and settled by more than two million blacks, half of them unofficially. People are jammed together in a variety of corrugated iron shacks and three- or four-room brick houses. Soweto has minimal or nonexistent street lighting. Outdoor plumbing and sewers overflow into the streets during rain storms. Blacks live five to a room, and smoke from a thousand shanty stacks lies like a heavy pall over the township day and night. Only the high veldt winds of August briefly disperse those clouds of acrid smoke.

In this cesspool of human squalor, robberies and rape are daily occurrences. In frustration and rage, and without always knowing why, blacks attack other blacks. Denied any kind of valid self-expression the people lose the capacity to love themselves and instead turn to violence—toward themselves and toward their neighbors.

Here can be found the infamous men's hostels which daily feed black labor into the city of Johannesburg. It is here that blacks are born, raised and educated to speak not only their own language but also English and Afrikaans, only to be sent out to work in the mines, or as messenger "boys," office cleaners and cheap labor for municipalities and private enterprises run by whites.

Sixty-four per cent of South Africa's economy is tied to importing and exporting activities, with most profits benefiting the white; very little trickles down to the blacks. The average per capita income for whites in South Africa today is $10,000; for blacks, it is a mere $1,000. The inequity is beyond belief.

My maternal grandfather, like many blacks of his generation, came to Johannesburg out of the need to earn money. In the 1920s, the government required Africans to begin paying taxes with hard currency instead of livestock or agricultural produce. In addition, the marketing infrastructure began to favor the white farmer by denying black villagers access to markets, thus making it impossible for the blacks to convert their crops into cash. The resulting black migration to the cities ensured a source of cheap black labor for the growing white-owned industries.

Like many before him, my grandfather left his family behind in a village in the rural area of Boons, sixty miles west of Johannesburg. My grandmother, who was not allowed to move with him, would visit from time to time. All their children—my mother, her four sisters and two brothers—were born in Boons.

My grandparents on my father's side came to Johannesburg at the end of the last century to work in the gold mines. They settled in the black enclave called Roodeport West, which became a satellite town on the west side of Johannesburg.

My father was born in a section of the town that was used to quarantine tuberculosis patients. I attribute his parents' early deaths to the fact that they lived in the squalor of the TB colony.

Because of my grandfather's dogged determination to pull his family out of the squalor of this TB colony, he systematically arranged for the education of his four sons. His plan required sacrificial giving on the part of all the children, and it was geared to ensuring that the youngest got the best education.

My father's oldest brother attended school until he reached standard six and could read and write and was then employable. At that point, he went to work as a clerk to help pay the school fees for his three brothers.

Because of the additional income, the second oldest was able to go further in his education—to standard nine—before he also left school to work. My father, the third in line, was not only able to finish standard nine, but went on to teacher-training college. It was at the beginning of my father's final year in college that my grandfather died. In order to pay for his final school year, my father had to sell some of my grandfather's clothes.

My father later married and settled in Roodeport West, and it was in this town that his children were born. Our values and outlook on life were deeply influenced by my father's love and respect for education. My drive and determination to succeed came from my parents' desire for a better life for themselves and their children.

We were a close-knit family that cared deeply for one another, wanted the best for each other and desperately wanted to do better than the previous generation. Above all, we were a family that wanted to be free from the yoke of the white man and to establish our own identity.

As I grew up, I regularly visited the village of my mother's family, which was near Roodeport West. I and my brothers

21

and sisters grew to love that village of Boons. It was clean, the air and food were of the highest quality, and most of the villagers enjoyed good health. None of the white man's diseases and smog-filled labor camps were to be found here. Boons was an idyllic location on the veldt.

My maternal grandfather and his people lived there for more than eighty years. They prided themselves that they had bought and paid for this land with their own sweat, and they had the title deeds signed by Paul Kruger to prove it.

When the government declared Boons a white spot, bitter resistance against the threat of forced removal began. My grandfather was one of twelve village elders who knew where the title deeds were hidden, but he refused to say. Had he revealed their whereabouts, the deeds would have been confiscated. My grandfather was not prepared to risk that, even though he knew that he would be caught up in a conflict with the local white magistrate, who was expected to enforce the removal of the village.

It wasn't long before the village elders were arrested and detained for questioning. The white regime was determined to get the title deeds and remove the tribe at all costs. However, the elders were even more determined to withstand any pressure in order to retain their ownership of the land. And so began six years of bitter conflict.

I remember sitting around an open hearth fire as a child, listening to my grandfather recall the horrors of detention and wondering whether the elders would have enough strength to resist disclosing the whereabouts of the title deeds. It was abundantly clear to us that my grandfather was determined to go to the grave with his secret if necessary. He ultimately did.

During those six years, the elders were periodically detained by the government, which tried to break their will and force them to sign title transfer agreements. While the elders were being held, the government tried to create division among the villagers by convincing them that there was no future for them in Boons, and at the same time promising incentives if they agreed to move.

They managed to convince a small minority of villagers to move, but the majority remained. It became obvious to the government that this strategy would not work.

As part of a new tactic, the government bulldozed the village school buildings to the ground, hoping this would force the villagers to move. However, the villagers then moved into the standing church buildings to educate their children. Enraged, the government bulldozed the church buildings.

What finally forced the villagers to move was the day government troops detained the elders for the last time. When the last elder had been rounded up, the troops destroyed the water-supply system. The government then told the people that they would demolish their homes and furniture unless the villagers agreed to move. Broken, defeated and without leaders, the villagers sadly loaded their few possessions onto army trucks and were driven to the homeland of Bophutatswana. When my grandfather and the other elders were finally released from detention, they were forcibly moved to the new settlement.

The government loaned each family two army tents for three months: one tent to cover their belongings and the other to live in. In those three months, the villagers were expected to build new houses because the army would need the tents to repeat the same operation elsewhere. Because the government refused to compensate them for their destroyed homes, the people did not have money to build houses. The Homeland settlement remained a shantytown for more than a decade.

As a result of brutal treatment during the numerous detentions, my grandfather could no longer do physical work. He was regularly detained for periods of six months at a time without charges laid against him and with no trial. Often during those detentions, he was tied for an entire day to a pole in the prison yard, stark naked in the tremendous heat of Pretoria.

My grandfather died in 1977 at the age of seventy-one, a disillusioned and bitter old man. He never revealed the whereabouts of the title deeds to the land. To this day the deeds lie buried somewhere under the soil. The government has never paid for nor held title deeds to the land.

These events created in me an early hatred for the white man and the system he represented.

My parents, too, had been forcibly moved from Roodeport to Soweto. The apartheid policies of the South African government produced this jumble of black townships called Soweto, where neighborhoods were ghettos of crime, witchcraft, street gangs, music and a culture dominated by soccer. It was into this scene that we eleven Molebatsi children arrived. At the tender age of twelve, I was about to encounter the ugliness of apartheid firsthand.

We Molebatsis prided ourselves on our ability to speak English at an early age. This skill placed us among a small group of people who could communicate in areas of economics, literature and, above all, political philosophy. We were forced to learn Afrikaans also, in order to address our white masters in their native tongue. In addition, we often used our native dialect—which whites could not understand. In our language skills, we were superior to most white families.

It was my use of language in a railway station that provoked my first personal experience of apartheid. The incident occurred as I waited to take a train from Ottosdaal to Wolmaranstad following a visit to relatives. These were two small towns in the Western Transvaal totally dominated by the white Afrikaners. The ticket clerk was, predictably, an Afrikaner; that sort of job was never given to a black.

I casually approached the counter and asked for a ticket. I had hardly finished speaking when the ticket clerk looked up at me and said, "What did you call me?" I had used the term "Meneer," an Afrikaans word that meant "Mister."

"Don't you dare call me 'mister'," screamed the ticket clerk. "That is how you speak to your kaffir preacher. You

24

call me 'Baas.' " With uncontrolled rage, he leaped from behind the counter, grabbed a large leather whip from the wall and lashed out in my direction.

I froze. My mouth dropped open and I began to shake all over. Then I turned and ran as fast as I could down the station passageway, bumping people as I ran.

Within seconds, the chase was joined by a uniformed white policeman. The two set after me in earnest. In a desperate effort to escape, I tore across the railroad tracks. It was futile; in the loose gravel I stumbled and fell.

Suddenly the policeman was on top of me, hauling me up by the scruff of the neck. He asked the clerk what the problem was, and my lack of respect was quickly explained. The policeman looked at me and said, "What are you waiting for? Ask the Baas to pardon you, and I'll ask the Baas not to beat you."

I had no choice. Either I apologized, or the clerk would whip the daylights out of me. Knowing how powerless I was, I apologized. The Baas had had his way.

An uneasy peace descended on the train station. In front of everyone I purchased my ticket and waited for what seemed hours for train to come. I had been shamed in front of my fellow blacks, and there was nothing they or I could do about it. They knew that my shame was their shame, and they shared my hurt and humiliation. But nobody said anything.

I had escaped punishment, but I was left with a deep sense of personal violation. I had been humiliated in front of dozens of my people and I had no recourse but to accept it. I wanted to scream my rage to the whole station. I found myself even hating my fellow blacks. By their inaction they, too, had caved in to the white man; they, too, had been humiliated.

Finally, the train arrived and I stepped aboard. As we moved away, I looked back at the station with loathing. With each passing kilometer, I tried to put emotional distance between myself and what had happened. But physical distance could not separate me from my sense of humiliation. That experience stayed with me. It often became a nightmare that woke me from my sleep. Even today when I take a train I am reminded of that ugly experience.

Years after the incident, as part of my own healing, I returned to that station. Of course the people had changed, and the ticket clerk was long gone. But that station still looked the same to me, still held all the awful memories of my humiliation. Standing there as a mature man, I realized that this experience had been my first lesson in personal hatred. I discovered that what I feared I also quickly learned to hate.

The extent to which my people and I were dehumanized revealed itself sharply in the way white people referred to themselves in the third person when talking to blacks. Once I nearly lost the meager income of 1.85 rand (about $.80) plus the four rand (about $2.00) I made in tips for a day's work at a supermarket because I refused to respect that dehumanizing practice.

A woman who was the floor manager at the store would often say to me, speaking of herself, "Boy, the missis wants you to bring that box of tomatoes and put it on the counter for the missis." ("Missis" was the feminine equivalent of "Baas.")

The way she addressed herself in the third person constantly humiliated me and reminded me of how utterly worthless I was in her eyes. I committed the unpardonable sin of asking why she referred to herself in the third person while I was standing right in front of her.

As far as she was concerned this amounted to my being a cheeky black. She flew into a rage and stormed off to the manager's office. I knew my head was about to roll.

Within minutes I was called into the office. The manager wordlessly handed me an envelope with 1.85 rand in it—no tip included. I was fired.

Mrs. Thomas, an English employee at the store, witnessed the entire episode. She saw me leave the office and noted that I had taken off my company-supplied apron. She asked me to wait and walked into the manager's office. Within minutes,

26

she emerged and told me that I didn't have to leave but that I was being transferred to another section of the store. I had received a temporary reprieve.

Despite the reprieve, I knew that nothing had really changed. My employment at the store did not last long. Soon after that incident I began to look for another job.

Ten years later, when I was twenty-seven and had returned to South Africa after five years in the United States, I discovered that time had not changed things in my homeland.

I was in a bank, waiting in line for a teller to serve me. Waiting in front of me in the same line was a woman who had taught me my first ABCs in school and whom I greatly respected. As we chatted and waited, I observed the way the bank staff was organized.

Of the five tellers, one was designated for blacks only, the other four waited on whites. During certain times of the day in large cities and small towns like Roodeport, black runners were assigned to bring in and bank the cash from small white-owned businesses and shops. These black runners would often have to stand in line for an hour or more, forfeiting their lunch in order to be served by a single teller—even though the four other tellers had no one to serve.

On this particular day, the four "whites-only" tellers had short lines. I was waiting in the "blacks-only" line with more than twenty people ahead of me. I grew progressively angry as I saw several of the other tellers standing idle, doing nothing.

The teller for our queue was no more than nineteen or twenty years old, and he was quite slow. It was bank policy to train inexperienced white boys on the blacks, for whom they thought quality service was not important.

When my former teacher finally approached the young man behind the counter, she said, "Baas, I would like this money to—" Before she had time to finish the sentence, I broke in and angrily said, "Why do you call this boy, 'Baas'?

27

He's younger than you and I, and you call him 'Baas'?"

She turned to me and said, "My son, if I don't call him 'Baas,' I'll never get served."

I could not bear to see her subservience, especially because she had once taught me the need for self-respect. I was so angry that I abruptly turned around and stomped across the bank to one of the "whites-only" lines and, through clenched teeth, ordered the woman teller to give me change. I put my money on the counter and said, "You are available. It's your job. Give me change."

She became angry and threw several packets of rolled coins onto the floor. The packets broke open and coins rolled in all directions behind the counter.

The bank grew deathly quiet; everybody stared at me. Suddenly I realized that I had crossed the line, had gone too far. I had made myself vulnerable to white attack, so I quickly went on the offensive.

I moved as fast as I could to the bank's public-relations booth. I looked the white public-relations officer straight in the eye and said, "I've had enough. I have my bank account here. I opened it while studying in the United States. And I have international accounts as well. I'm not going to take any nonsense from her or from anyone else in this bank."

I was calling his bluff. At the same time I knew that a black man with overseas experience might have leverage, and there would be a degree of caution on their part in dealing with me. Meanwhile, the woman teller continued her ranting and raving.

At that point, the bank manager stepped out of his office at the back of the bank and saw the woman kneeling to pick up the scattered coins.

All of a sudden, the whole scene struck me as hilarious—my own anger, the bewildered public-relations officer, the ranting teller, the startled customers, the confused bank manager—and I started to laugh.

When I regained my composure, I quickly took advantage of the manager's ignorance of what had happened. Innocently, I told him that all I wanted was to get change.

No doubt anxious to get me out of his bank and put things back to normal, the manager ordered the public-relations officer to take care of me. In no time, I had my change and was standing outside on the street.

My former teacher was waiting outside, obviously wondering what had happened to me. She breathed a sigh of relief when she saw me walk out without handcuffs and with no signs of a beating.

While it had its humorous side, the incident demonstrated one of the many tragic results of apartheid. Blacks and whites alike have been conditioned to behave in a particular way—no matter whether or not that behavior serves the best personal or commercial interests. The irony of that situation was that it was in the best interests of the bank to serve all customers, black or white. Good business has no nationality or color attached to it.

3
A Brief History Lesson

The history of South Africa is the history of a black people before and after the white man's arrival. We preceded him and yet he is now part of the history of the southern tip of this vast continent.

My personal history is bound up in part with the white man's history. My life was independent of him, but became interwoven with him as his continued presence became an inevitability in my life and in the lives of all black people throughout southern Africa.

Black South African history since 1652 consists not only of the oft-spoken white dominance and the so-called civilizing of black people. Rather, it is a history of our people's resistance to the systematic dispossession of our land by whites.

In the seventeenth century the first European settlements were founded by English and Dutch visitors on their way to and from the Indies. The first twelve citizens settled on small farms along the Liesbeck River in 1657. Expansion soon followed.

In 1658 the first batch of slaves from the Dutch East Indies, Indonesia, and East Africa were brought in as skilled artisans to the Cape Malay community. In time the Khoisan, two tribes in the Cape area comprising the Khoi and San (both known as shepherding tribes), began to enter the employment of the settlers. Some did so because they had been deprived of their lands and cattle; others were attracted by the prospects of material gain. The Dutch settlers referred to them as Hottentots.

As white settlers moved north of the Cape they brought conflict with the Khoi. What started as friendship soon deteriorated as the Khoi realized what was happening to their lands in the hands of the settlers. Goods and land were being bartered off. Skirmishes in the form of guerrilla attacks took place against the settlers. War finally broke out.

With the deepening animosities came hardening racial attitudes. When the colony was first established there were obvious feelings of superiority over the Khoi. While open racial discrimination was not the policy, the whites clearly did not favor the tribe.

However, because men outnumbered women in the white colony, sexual relationships between the races became common. By 1671 three quarters of the children born to slave women at the Cape were of mixed descent.

Over time racial attitudes adopted by the Europeans hardened, and a large number of blacks, many of whom had adopted European culture, found fewer and fewer opportunities open to them.

The expansion of the colony, the arrival of more European settlers and the constant struggle for ownership of the land only increased racial hostilities. By the 1800s, the British had assumed the government of the land, and the Dutch (known as the Boers) realized they had no political power. Unhappy with the British and their laws, the Boers left the Cape and traveled north and inland, beginning what became known as the Great Trek.

The lands beyond the Cape colony's borders were owned and populated by the Xhosa and Zulu. As the Boers advanced, it was inevitable that conflict would occur. On December 16, 1838, 500 Boers met 10,000 Zulus at Blood River. The Boers formed a defensive circle with their wagons and killed 3,000 Zulus, suffering only three casualties themselves. The Boers settled on the land they had won from the Zulu and established the republic of Natalia. However, in 1842 the British invaded Natalia and the Dutch

32

were once again under British rule.

The settlement of our tribal lands by the advancing Boers took place with little resistance. In the Dutch flight from the British Empire, the African tribes along the way showed kindness to the travelers, providing them with food and provisions so they would not starve. Our kindness was our undoing. When the Boers gained power, we became second-class citizens in our own land.

The Dutch established several Boer republics which were to be independent from British rule. Black people were a non-issue in this process, not even considered worthy to be negotiated with. It became a struggle solely between the Boer and the Briton. It was a case of two elephants fighting for territory, crushing the grass beneath their feet. Blacks were the grass under the ruling white elephant feet.

In 1844 the Dutch established the South African Republic, with their capital at Pretoria. Here they faced no interference from the British. By the 1860s, South Africa was divided into British and Dutch Afrikaner regions, with only a few areas remaining under black or coloured control. It was the beginning of the end for my people.

In the late 1800s, the English began to develop the mining industry. Boom towns sprang up along the Reef. With lands gone and traditional black leaders now accountable to their new white rulers, many disillusioned blacks turned to the squalor of the mining camps around Johannesburg.

It was into these circumstances that my paternal grandfather was forced to work for the white man in the mining town of Roodeport. Thrust into this culturally and ethnically diverse situation my grandfather found himself mixing with people from other tribes.

As a result he married Adellinah, a woman from another tribe. It was a happy marriage that produced five children. But it was to be a life of estrangement and servitude, dominated by laws and regulations imposed on him, and by a system that totally ignored his rights and the kind of government he had grown up with. This foreign government called him an alien and separated him from his tribal past and his land in ways that would slowly dehumanize him.

The turning point for my people had begun. The downward spiral of humiliation was now set in place and the patterns of abuse would create generations of learned helplessness. Blacks as a people—and my family in particular—would, for the next two generations, cooperate in our own oppression.

The Anglo-Boer war of 1899 brought to a climax the tensions between the British Cape government and the Dutch who had settled in the Boer republics of the north. Strictly speaking, it was a South African war, because many blacks took part in it.

The four-year war ended with a victory for the British. English-speaking South Africans remained firmly in control of both economic and political power.

In 1910 the Union of South Africa was formed from the four existing colonies. All black South Africans, except those in the Cape, were excluded from the vote. In reaction, a number of black leaders including chiefs, lawyers, teachers and clergymen formed a unified political organization of their own. They met in Bloemfontein in 1912 and formed the South African Native National Congress. The name was later changed to the African National Congress (ANC), a group devoted to a nonracial South Africa. This union, however, did not put blacks on an equal standing with the British. Blacks, Indians and Malays were still left out in the political wilderness with nowhere to go.

The beginning of the end for black freedoms came in 1913 when parliament passed the Native Land Act, one of the most important parliamentary acts in South African history. This legislation laid the foundation for modern segregation. It effectively divided the Union of South Africa into areas for blacks and areas for whites. It restricted black ownership and possession to a very small part of the land. In the final break-up of the land, Europeans took eighty-seven per cent of the land, leaving a mere thirteen per cent, mostly non-arable land, for Africans. The reality was even worse; blacks actually were allowed to occupy only slightly more than seven per cent of the land.

The result of the Native Land Act was to make black farming on white-owned land illegal. Blacks were now isolated not only from the political process but also from the land that was once theirs.

In 1923 the government passed the Natives (Urban Areas) Act which set up black townships outside the major cities. The land in these townships was owned by the government, and blacks could only rent homes and not buy them. The point of the law was clear: blacks were considered temporary visitors, to be held at arm's length from the white cities.

By the early 1900s, then, the situation in South Africa was one of legalized racial discrimination.

During this period it became apparent to Afrikaners that they must organize themselves if they were ever going to achieve economic prosperity in their adopted land. In the end, it took thirty years and a political philosophy of self-determination—which included doing business only among themselves, having large families and promoting only those who had committed themselves to the Afrikaner advancement—to achieve the success they sought.

Once established, Afrikaners were a majority of the white population. They rode to power on the crest of a wave of Afrikaner nationalism that was both anti-British and anti-black. A new Afrikaner government, headed by a former Boer general, instituted laws that established separate black townships and barred black workers from collective bargaining. Blacks were denied further political rights.

But divisions were also beginning to form among the Afrikaners themselves, fanned by the worldwide economic depression of the 1930s. A split in the Afrikaner political parties led to the rise of the Purified National Party, later called the National Party.

While the English were preoccupied with commerce and industry, the Nationalist Party gained political power. On May 26, 1948, the Nationalist Party became the ruling party.

The year 1948 also marked another milestone in South African history. It was the year apartheid was born, making racism the official law of the land.

4
A Victory for Apartheid

When Dr. D. F. Malan took office as the first prime minister under apartheid in 1948, the legislative program was in place to enshrine the principle of divide and rule.

English government officials were summarily dismissed and replaced overnight by Afrikaners regardless of their competency. In no time at all significant government departments were controlled by ideologically "safe" bureaucrats. Over the next five years a vigorous legislative program followed that entrenched the idea of the separation of the races into permanent racial structures.

Apartheid envisioned a society in which each race lived entirely apart—separate homes, separate jobs, separate churches, separate theaters and restaurants. No racial mixing of any kind would be allowed—especially not in marriage. Blacks could enter white areas only to sell their services as laborers. After that, they were required to return to their own areas, which were specified on the passes that black men were to carry at all times. It was truly a case of divide and rule. We were divided and they ruled.

No black family escaped the devastating consequences of these laws. And one of the most devastating laws was the Bantu Education Act, proposed in 1953 and formally adopted in 1955.

Hitherto the English, largely Anglican, church had resisted serving the designs and policies of the government and had involved itself in ministering to the poor and downtrodden, largely through education.

But the apartheid government needed the church to undergird its new designs to separate and safeguard the survival of the Afrikaner. To do this, the church needed to be diverted from its mission to educate and to serve and uphold the basic needs of the poor within the framework of the gospel.

Instead, the state wanted the church to focus solely on spiritual needs. By so doing, the government could snatch away the educational system the church had built up over a century and bring it under the state's control. This they succeeded in doing through the Bantu Education Act.

This act gave the government the absolute power it needed to control what the black man could and could not be trained to do. In the words of the first minister of Bantu Education, Dr. Hendrik Verwoerd, "What is the use of teaching a Bantu child mathematics when he cannot use it in practice..? It is therefore necessary that native education should be controlled in such a way that it should be in accordance with the policy of the state." The prospect of me and my siblings receiving the kind of education my father wanted for us was dashed.

With the passing of the act, education was set to produce a subservient black whose sole purpose was to serve the predetermined interests of the white community.

It had two major objectives: First, it was designed to give only the most basic literacy and math skills to the new army of industrial workers. Second, it was intended to discipline the rebellious youth of the townships. What it in fact did was introduce mass schooling of a very basic and inferior kind. The Bantu Education Act lowered educational standards because the white government had no interest in seeing the black man succeed. If he did he might have political aspirations, which were the sole preserve of the white ruling class.

The purpose of black education now was to create a working class for the white economic system, thus ensuring a standard of living superior to anything on the African continent. The black man was to be dependent forever on the white man's largesse. It was the purest and most subtle form of racial genocide.

My father, a teacher at heart, found himself caught in a viselike no-win situation. Should he continue to teach under the new act, helping the children who desperately needed an education, or should he boycott the whole system—with no alternative in sight? Many teachers, including my father, opted to stay. Together they formed organizations like the Transvaal Union of African Teachers to voice their opposition to the new educational philosophy. They also continued to be active members in black liberation movements.

Simultaneously with the new education act came the Group Areas Act, which enabled the government to consolidate black residential areas.

The old home where we had lived in Roodeport West was now considered too close to the white community. We were thought to pose a threat to the poor whites who lived nearest to us: in the event that the government needed to control riots in the black township, these whites would easily be caught in the crossfire.

So to conform to the new policy of a buffer zone, the races were kept separate by a strip of unoccupied land 12 kilometers (4 and a half miles) wide—a sort of no man's land without mines.

As a result my family of thirteen was forcibly moved from Roodeport West, where we had owned both our home and the land under it, to Dobsonville, a suburb of Soweto where we were jammed into a two-bedroom house. The police and army now had access to our home any time of the day or night on any pretext. The army could be called in at a moment's notice to seal off the four roads leading in and out of Soweto, thereby confining more than two million of my people. Water and electricity could be cut instantly, and delivery of food to the township choked. All this could be achieved in less than an hour.

An even darker side of the Group Areas Act allowed low-level bureaucrats to create and control the activities of people in the concentration-camp atmosphere of townships like Soweto.

For example, each household was required by the Influx Control Laws to have a permit indicating who lived in the house. New permits were issued only to immediate family members, not the extended family of African cultural tradition. Anyone found in our home by the police who was not on the permit would automatically be arrested for trespassing. These raids were carried out indiscriminately, and they became a means of harassing those people whom the local officials considered agitators.

This law directly impacted my family. My father, being a schoolteacher, was often expected to have other family members stay with us who were less fortunate and, more often than not, impoverished. This automatically violated the Influx Control Laws act. At one point, one of my aunts was living with us until she married. Every late-night knock at the door raised the level of our anxiety.

The last major problem which confronted the black urban population in the late 1950s came when the government forced African women to apply for and carry pass books in the same way that black males did. Huge demonstrations were organized by the ANC all over the country, and leaders like Albert Luthuli led campaigns in which men and women burned their passes in public.

One demonstration against this inhumanity was the historic march to Pretoria by 20,000 women. Rural women are the most vulnerable in South Africa, as they do not have the organizational structures that exist in the townships. But even in rural areas resistance was evident. Gradually, the relentless application of the laws broke down their resolve. Women in the small towns fell next. Finally women in the new townships, who had only recently arrived there, caved in.

The anti-pass campaigns reached their peak in 1960. Campaigns launched by the ANC and the Pan-African Congress (PAC), an organization in pursuit of a pure black society, an "Africa for the Africans," led to a violent outburst at Sharpeville, in the Transvaal area. On March 21, police opened fire on the demonstrators, killing 69 people and wounding 178. The struggle between black and white was now marked by terrorism on the one hand and brute force on the other. The result was the government's declaration of the first state of emergency.

This gave the cabinet ministers of the apartheid government awesome powers. The application of these emergency laws led to the banning of the ANC and PAC and started an historical chain of events that has since made the Afrikaner the prisoner of his own dogma.

The banning of these two organizations demonstrated to many that the white government was not interested in negotiating with reasonable people; the cause of black political rights would be decided on the battlefield. This led the ANC and PAC to go underground, their leaders becoming fugitives. Both groups established military branches and began training their people in secret bases to be guerilla fighters. They succeeded in acts of sabotage that included blowing up power stations, post offices and railway junctions, as well as cutting telephone lines. Many blacks despaired and thousands turned their backs on what seemed to be a futile struggle. Dozens of black leaders were arrested and many more fled into exile.

My family, which had been forcibly deposited in Soweto, now found itself in a dilemma. Apart from all the ideological developments, the black townships had become places where gangs, squalor and despair contrasted with the quiet of the villages. We could either stay in Soweto at some personal risk, and confront all the black ideological developments which demanded a commitment and more suffering than we were prepared for, or migrate to the nearest village.

As a compromise we stayed in Soweto and my father traveled to the village to teach. At the same time he looked for a permanent home for us all. That was a tall order for someone with a family of thirteen.

A decade of uneasy quiet descended on black political activity within South Africa. It seemed as if people wanted to forget the Sharpeville Massacre and the life sentences handed down to Nelson Mandela and other ANC and PAC leaders.

The African thinking of the early 1950s reformed and emerged in the form of the Black Consciousness movement in the early seventies. This time it was spearheaded by aggressive and highly motivated black university students. Their speeches rekindled the passion for freedom and the right of the black man to determine and control his own destiny. The black universities became the powerhouses for new thinkers and new leaders.

One such leader was Steven Biko. His writings and speeches broke new ground. In 1968 he and a group of fellow black students formed the South African Students' Organization (SASO), which stressed pride and independence for black people. Organizations like COSAS (Congress of South African Students), and later AZAPO (Azanian Peoples Organization), sprang up and influenced a new generation of young blacks.

Biko died in 1977 at the hands of the secret police. His death brought many people to a moment of decision about their personal involvement in the struggle for liberation. The white security system had proven itself incapable of listening to reasonable people. The option to join the armed struggle seemed to be the only logical choice for many.

5
The White Man's God

Any knowledge I had of God had come largely through a church that was controlled by whites.

The white man's God came into our lives because of my father's involvement in the Anglican church. My father had been a Sunday school superintendent, but his involvement was more a matter of conformity to social convention than a deeply felt faith in what the church taught. With the enactment of the Bantu Education Act, even that involvement ended. The Anglican church failed to speak out against the discriminating legislation, and my father was forced to ask himself how he could associate with this church.

The day the legislation was passed my father waited for the English church and community to protest. He searched anxiously through the newspapers and waited by the radio. But no English voices were raised in protest. The English-speaking community and the church he had faithfully served all his life had betrayed him. On that bitterly cold day he quit organized religion. He was not to darken the door of any church again for more than twenty years, when my father would become a believer in a much deeper sense.

I identified with my father's feelings, but my own disillusionment with the church had begun much earlier. By the time I was a teenager, the rituals, prayers and sermons failed to stir a single emotional impulse or religious response in me. I saw the church as an unnecessary social appendage.

Our family continued to pay our dues to the church by attending occasional services at Christmas or Easter. But this

43

attendance was only a means to secure the residency status documentation required by the government. Because we lived in the township, we needed always to carry proof of who we were, where we had been born and what schools we attended. A baptismal or confirmation certificate provided by the church was acceptable documentation in the eyes of the government. So it was personally and politically wise for blacks to maintain some semblance of involvement with the church. However, such involvement had nothing to do with real, living faith.

The church had brought its Bible to our shores, but now that church and its Bible were being used to justify and maintain the policy of apartheid. The church had come to the natives preaching the Bible's message of good news and peace, but whenever the natives got restless, the Bible became a club to beat blacks into submission and obedience to the whites.

The thirteenth chapter of the Bible's book of Romans was frequently used to crush any thoughts of civil disobedience. In this chapter, St. Paul writes: "Everyone must submit himself to the governing authorities, for there is no authority except that which God has established. The authorities that exist have been established by God. Consequently, he who rebels against the authority is rebelling against what God has instituted, and those who do so will bring judgment on themselves."

When we failed to "submit" or showed signs of rebelling, white Dutch Reformed clergymen used this passage to explain and justify the government's brutal oppression and retaliation. The same clergymen labeled black leaders of the resistance movements "unchristian," because they refused to submit to injustices imposed by the governing authorities. These clergymen wanted us to believe that submission demanded blind obedience to the state, no matter how evil and immoral the policies of the state proved to be. It never occurred to them that God also demands justice from the state—and not just justice for whites. Nor did they consider that the Bible gives us the right to oppose injustice. To "submit" does not imply blind obedience as the whites wanted us to believe. They also turned conveniently away from the injunction that the ruler is "God's servant for your good." What happens when that rule is no longer good for the majority of the people?

Sadly, even black ministers preached the same perverted message, trying to pacify us with soothing talk of God's love while, at the same time, condemning legitimate aspirations of our people. Such double messages confused us. However, for many years the church was able to achieve its objective; blacks submitted and conformed to the status quo.

The educational system's portrait of God was no better. Like all my fellow students, I was forced to sit week after week through a dull religious-education class because it was a required subject in high school. Religious education was viewed as a way to make us passive and to create good, conforming citizens of the state. Ironically, we were never allowed to be true citizens: we had no voting rights, we could not travel, and we could never own a passport. We were aliens in our own land. The religion lessons were irrelevant to the reality of our daily lives.

The government's insistence that we study the Bible in school ultimately backfired. It was in our Bible studies that we read Old Testament prophets such as Amos who condemned the Israelites for their injustice, and their oppression of the poor and needy. And we discovered how God punished this injustice by allowing the Israelites to be conquered and taken into exile. What was the difference, I thought, between the Israelites' acts of oppression and injustice and what the Afrikaner government was doing to blacks in the Homelands and in the urban areas of South Africa? The more I thought about these Bible readings, the more convinced I became that the government's system of apartheid was evil.

What angered me most was the way the government and the churches misused the Bible to justify this demonic

45

system. Their efforts to convince the black population that apartheid policies were motivated by Christian principles rankled me deeply. It was an obvious lie, but a lie perpetuated so forcefully that, after a while, it came to be accepted as true by most whites and even by many blacks.

I recall one day being visited in our home by two well-meaning white Dutch Reformed church missionaries who wanted to discuss with my father his "ordained" place in the segregated society they had created and to explain why he was only a second-class citizen in it. My father graciously ushered them into the dining room and closed the door, excluding the rest of the family from the discussion. He heard them out, and then the missionaries left. No voices were raised.

My father had made sure we children were not present during the discussions because he knew we would embarrass the visitors with aggressive talk about issues of equality and racial discrimination. My father was a gentleman to the end.

Deep inside the Afrikaner mind is the belief that apartheid—the separation of the races—has biblical sanction. Various Old Testament passages are constantly used to defend apartheid. The Afrikaners defend their attitudes that blacks are inferior, and therefore should be kept separate from whites, by citing the Old Testament story in which Noah curses his son and his son's descendants (the Canaanites): "Cursed be Canaan! The lowest of slaves will he be to his brothers." According to the Afrikaner, blacks are descendants of Canaan; the curse of slavery and oppression is ours by inheritance. This is a twisted interpretation and blatant misuse of Scripture for political ends.

To set forth their position, the Dutch Reformed churches in the 1950s poured out a mountain of literature explaining their theological basis for apartheid. This position was supported by the South African Bureau for Racial Affairs (SABRA) a think tank on race policy. So it came as an acute embarrassment when, in 1986, the main Dutch Reformed church (NGK) declared that this position regarding apartheid was heresy. Such a position had been attempted before. In 1960, the NGK had declared that "no one who believes in Jesus Christ may be excluded from any church on the grounds of his color or race." This so enraged Prime Minister Hendrik Verwoerd that the Dutch Reformed church leadership recanted. But this could not stop the flow of events that led to the World Alliance of Reformed Churches in Ottawa, Canada, declaring apartheid an "evil ideology" and a "pseudoreligious ideology." In 1986, the NGK once and for all declared apartheid a "heresy." This time it stuck.

The embarrassing mood of dissent over apartheid was heightened when Dr. Beyers Naude, the son of Dr. Joshua Naude, a well-known and zealous Afrikaner nationalist, broke with his father's beliefs and began a long struggle against apartheid. His actions resulted in his resignation from the Dutch Reformed church and the founding of the Christian Institute, an organization established in response to the conflict between church and government.

Other voices were also beginning to be heard in South Africa. Among them was Reverend Desmond Tutu, who rose to prominence first among Anglicans and then as a spokesman for the silenced leadership of the Mass Democratic Movement (MDM), an umbrella movement that brought together Afrikaner dissidents to form a grand opposition alliance.

But pressures from the outside world were also beginning to be felt, first from religious groups like the World Council of Churches and then from the United Nations. Suddenly the voice of the church in South Africa was being heard, and the voice of the Anglican Church was among the loudest.

There remains a standing joke among blacks that white, English-speaking South African Christians hate two things. The first is apartheid, the second is blacks. The fair-minded British hate apartheid in theory, and they loudly vocalize this hatred. But they are not eager to deny themselves the advantages and privileges they have reaped from the system. Apartheid enables them to keep their schools, hospitals and universities exclusively white, and it allows them to practice the same kind of wage discrimination as the Afrikaners who openly espouse apartheid.

Churches, too, are not immune to the lull of the status quo. For years, mainline denominations in South Africa included both blacks and whites in their national membership rolls. However, membership in individual congregations was based on race. There were "black churches" and "white churches," and these racial lines were almost never crossed. The black priests and ministers who served the black congregations rarely addressed political issues or social involvement.

The missionary churches were little different. They were basically pietistic, otherworldly communities without any relevance to the black situation. Black pastors emerging from these churches were financed by white, western missionary societies and parroted the theology of these mission societies. Blacks were given no reason to believe that there was a way out of the ghetto, let alone to think that God might be interested in their freedom and dignity. These churches became known for their revivalist tent meetings. While the singing and dancing were African in form, the churches gave very little thought to key issues that controlled the lives of black Africans. Personal salvation was fervently preached, but to the exclusion of God's concern for the plight of the poor and oppressed. Christianity was offered as an insurance policy for the afterlife; life on earth was not related to the message of salvation. The black pastors both taught and were taught that it was all right to suffer now because they could look forward to streets of gold in heaven. Meanwhile, white people could have their gold here and now—and, presumably, also in the hereafter. Black evangelists turned a blind eye to their brothers' suffering.

My father reacted negatively to the mainline denominations, but he held a particular disdain for the missionary churches. He saw them as nothing more than a tool in the hands of neo-colonialists. He discouraged me and my brothers from having anything to do with this kind of church. This attitude deeply imbedded itself in my young mind. For my father, the fundamental issue in South Africa was apartheid: to resolve this problem was to resolve everything else. Any religion that did not address this central problem was a waste of time. When the English church failed to address the issue of apartheid, my father dismissed it. My brothers and I followed our father's example; we left the church with no intention of ever returning.

6
A Time of Hope

The months that followed my Christmas Eve accident and the subsequent loss of my leg were filled with feelings of anger and vengeance. I could not shake the feeling that I was owed justice, and my feelings turned anger into action. My brother George and I set the day and the hour when we would burn down the home of the man who almost killed me. But events in my life were about to take a radically different direction—a turn in the road I had not charted or anticipated.

It all started after I returned to school. I was still on crutches, still angry and anxious about how my fellow students would react to my new disability. I doubted my ability to cope, but I had a desire to try to make things work out.

During my first weeks back I met an outspoken young man with very decided opinions about life. His name was Diamond Atong.

Diamond was a confirmed Christian but he was not just another big mouth on campus, like so many of the "holier than thou" Christians who were our contemporaries. His deeds matched his words. I learned that his nickname was "the Pope" because he always carried a New Testament that he read from to support his arguments about life's questions. The name suited him well. More often than not he was able to come up with good arguments as to why the Bible was true and why and how it could offer answers for everyday living.

Diamond was one of the outstanding members of the high-school debating team. He was a clear-headed, intelligent

51

young man who won most of his debates and was near the top of his class. I found it odd that he was intellectually far above average, and yet he saw no contradiction between the Bible and academic learning. As much as I wanted to, I could not easily ignore him.

We were on different teams in the debating society, and we would often find ourselves on opposite sides of various important subjects—especially on the subject of religion.

I frequently found myself in turmoil because he always seemed to have an answer from the Bible to most issues brought up in debate. Could there be an answer from the Bible to my question about why I had almost been killed by a white man? If so, would I be ready to accept it? Was there an answer to the problem of evil in the world; to oppression; to my own personal suffering? Would I always live with this burning hatred in my heart—even if I was successful in killing the driver of the car? I had no answers to these questions. I only knew I was beginning to doubt my own negative attitude toward the Bible.

I had my reasons for rejecting Christianity, reasons I thought Diamond never had to face. I was wrong. Diamond had all the reasons in the world, plus a lot more, to oppose God and faith. He had been abandoned by his father; his mother was forced into servitude on land owned by a cruel white farmer; and in his poverty he had contracted tuberculosis, which forced him to move to Soweto where he lived with his older brother and fifteen other family members in a two-bedroom house. Diamond's faith amazed me all the more as I discovered more about his life.

My father looked down on the church because he could see no difference between those who went and those who didn't. The men he worshipped with on Sunday morning would be like the devil on a holiday on Monday. The fact that they read the Bible and prayed on Sunday did not affect the way they behaved the rest of the week.

But Diamond was a different kind of Christian. He was the same no matter what the day of the week, no matter who he was with. He would invite me to various meetings to hear different speakers lecture on a variety of religious subjects. On one occasion a speaker addressed a group on the subject of the resurrection.

This was of particular interest to me because part of my body was now gone. The thought of a completely new and restored body both intrigued me and made me extremely skeptical at the same time. While I had often heard the story of Jesus' resurrection, the idea of someone dying and rising again always puzzled me. While Jesus' resurrection offered great hope, it also seemed to be the weakest link in the Christian faith.

As a biology student I knew that flesh and bones were subject to decay. It was an incredible leap of faith to think that disintegrated bodies could suddenly be restored physically. How could a dead man rise from the grave? I could quite possibly believe in the immortality of the soul, but to believe that a decayed mass of bones would one day be restored neither made sense nor fit the facts of the world as I perceived it.

As much as I rejected the whole idea of the dead rising, I was beginning to doubt my own unbelief. I could not stop thinking about the resurrection and the implications of it for my own life.

One day Mr. Nathaniel Nkosi, from an organization called Youth Alive, came to our school to speak to us. Word of his coming quickly spread around the campus. He was going to talk on the resurrection of the dead, a subject I had become somewhat familiar with by now. I decided I would go along and listen to him. On the day of his talk, I arrived early and stood at the back of the hall. I planned to ridicule him when he had finished. I was ready to hit him with the standard "contradictions in the Bible" speech that I had prepared and knew so well. My friends were primed, looking forward to my verbally putting this man in his place.

When Mr. Nkosi got up to speak, however, something changed my attitude. I just sat there and listened. I was strangely caught off-guard by this man's sincerity, something I had not counted on. In my mind I said, this man has not had much education, and yet he speaks with such utter conviction and simplicity about the resurrection of Jesus from the dead and our resurrection that I cannot ignore him. I found myself stunned into silence.

When he finished, he invited questions from the audience. My friends immediately looked in my direction, expecting me to cross-examine and ridicule the speaker. I was silent. I had nothing to say. My mouth was dry and I knew that my responses would ring hollow if I tried to contradict him. I left the meeting in silence, my friends looking at me in complete bewilderment.

A few weeks later Diamond invited me to come to a meeting of Youth Alive. Before we went, he tried to explain to me what it was all about. No matter how much he explained, I was not prepared for my first encounter. That meeting nearly turned me off altogether from giving Christianity any serious thought.

First, there were the extemporaneous prayers. Then there was the arrival of a white couple who seemed to be completely at home among these black young people. Prayers and white people in the same room brought to mind negative images of the white man's God.

The few times I had attended church, prayers were read from a written text and not spoken freely. Whenever I was called upon to read the prayers, I would do so in a stiff, formal fashion and then I would sit down. But the kind of prayer going on at Youth Alive was very different. People simply stood up from wherever they were and started praying, as though they had some special relationship with God and expected him to answer them. I thought to myself that that was either the height of folly or there was something here that was rather unusual, perhaps even true. Whatever it was, I had to find out. I wasn't prepared to dismiss it anymore.

And yet, up at the front sat those two white people. Despite their naturalness and unaffected ways it was too much for me to take. Their presence deeply irritated me. Then and there I made plans to leave. But I couldn't. I remained fixed to my seat.

Diamond suddenly stood up and introduced me to the group. A few minutes later we broke up into small groups. In the smaller group I found a real openness among these young people. I found myself relaxed enough to share my doubts about the resurrection, my experiences with white people and the accident that had almost killed me. They listened and seemed to understand my fears and feelings.

For the first time I was attending a religious meeting that was not a required high-school religious-instruction class nor was it being held in a church. These kids seemed to know what they were talking about and seemed to believe it with a passionate intensity I had not witnessed before. I left Youth Alive that evening with mixed feelings, but I was determined to give the organization—including the white couple—another chance.

As a result of my first experience at Youth Alive I began to attend on a regular basis. As I attended, I asked myself: am I being manipulated by their love or am I being drawn by something higher? Fortunately, I was given the opportunity to reflect on what I was hearing and to challenge it. A verse out of the book of Proverbs in the Old Testament hit me with great force: "There is a way that seems right unto a man, but the end thereof is the way of death." Was this verse speaking to me and to my rejection of God? Would my way only lead to death?

I found myself responding to something higher than myself. But was it God? I knew there was a need in my own life, but now it had nothing to do with my being a cripple or even with regard to the accident. I began to really reflect on God, who he was and what he stood for and how all this would impact my life if I came to really believe in him.

The emotions that had driven me for so long were hatred and rage, and they had served and motivated me well. In hating the white man I had established my self-image, my self-esteem. But now I was being challenged to love my enemy. That meant not only the two white people I met at Youth Alive but also the white man who had run me down. In fact, all white people.

I wrestled deeply with the question: How could I believe and practice the Bible's command to love my enemy after all I had suffered at the hands of white people? I had every reason to both hate and fear the white man. I wanted his destruction. And now I was being told to love him against every instinct inside myself. I asked myself again and again, Why? What had he ever done for me? Why should I love the oppressor?

The more I thought about all this, however, the less it seemed I could carry out my plan of revenge. Going to Youth Alive saved me not only from destroying a man's property, and perhaps his life and the lives of his family, but it also saved me from a fate that finally overtook my brother George. I don't believe I would be a free man today if I had gone through with my plan. As I look back I believe it was providence that kept me from murder and mayhem during that long, dark struggle between love and hate. My life was changing. Love was triumphing where hatred had reigned, and I found myself caught up in a power stronger than I could imagine or control. I was slowly being reborn.

I was changing in other ways as well. A chance meeting on our high-school campus with a social worker from the West Rand Cripple Care Association led to my first wooden leg.

If the Bible was beginning to change the way I saw God, the new leg was changing the way I saw myself. I saw life taking on new dimensions that I had not thought possible. People would not just stare at me or patronize me or feel pity for me anymore. On the inside I would be able to rebuild my dignity and self-esteem once again. I thanked the social worker with a cry of gratitude from my heart. She was just as overjoyed as I was.

It took me a single day to learn to walk on my new artificial leg. My father could barely contain himself. We both saw it as the beginning of a new life for me, and we had a family celebration to mark the occasion. I threw away my crutches and started walking on my own.

There were times in the early days when I slipped and fell, but I picked myself up and went on. I was at last on the road to self-sufficiency and wholeness. I knew deep in my heart that whatever awaited me in the future, I had rounded an important corner in my life and I would never look back again.

7

Youth Alive

In April 1967, at a Youth Alive retreat, I finally faced up to God and his claims on my life.

At the retreat I began earnestly to ask questions about God—who he was and how he would affect my life if I surrendered to him. What was my life all about? Where was I going? What if I had died the day of that accident in 1964; what would have been the significance of my life on this earth?

I also wrestled with my name. My father called me Caesar after the Roman emperor, and from the time I was a little boy the story of Julius Caesar was used to reinforce my father's desire for my life. "My boy," he would say, "you must be ambitious in life. You must achieve the great things that last, and they must overshadow the mistakes you might make." None of his sons should simply strive for equality with whites; we were meant to be greater than they were.

At that time I was quite a visionary. Politically I saw myself standing on a platform some day and really sounding off about the issues of the day. But at this particular time in my life there was only one haunting issue, the issue posed by the wise man Solomon in another time and culture: "There is a way that seems right unto a man, but the end thereof is the way of death."

I saw myself as an activist, an articulate educated activist, someone who could change the political face of South Africa if given the opportunity. In my mind political legislation was the only way to bring about change, and for black people to effect such legislation they must eradicate the "white pro-blem."

For outsiders, understanding oppression can be difficult. If you see it only in terms of written laws, it doesn't hit you as hard. But when you see it daily in terms of doors of opportunity slammed in your face, it's another matter.

Within the black community we were reduced to five or six professions. We could become schoolteachers, nurses, med-ical doctors, social workers, lawyers or clergymen. If we didn't want to be any of these six things, we couldn't be anything except hard labor for the white man. At this point I saw my life in stark terms, and that concerned me. What was I called to do?

Behind all my thinking lurked the white man's Bantu Education Act that said you must never educate an African beyond what he is going to be allowed to do in society. That sounded the death knell to any future for the Black man in South Africa. That piece of legislation really hit me very hard as a young man trying to work my way into society and onto the educational and vocational ladder.

Questions began to nag me. Was I going to make it? And what if I did make it? Would I be completely fulfilled, contented and satisfied? Suppose I *was* fulfilled in a career of my choosing; would it last? Would I be like the missile that shoots upward with a great roar, fills out the sky briefly and then disappears like a small stick on the horizon, with no life left in it? I found these questions deeply disturbing, and I knew that there was something missing in my life.

I was faced with a major decision that would affect all of my plans for the future. Would I identify with Christ regardless of the personal cost or would I go it alone? It had come down to that. While it did not answer other questions of what I would do with my life, or how or where I would live, I knew I was being confronted with the most momentous of life-changing decisions. On my answer would hinge the rest of my life.

It took me a long time to reach that decision point. I had

fought and struggled. I had studied. I had looked for what it meant for me and my people to be liberated from the white man. I looked forward to facing my foe on the political battlefield, of having a great and fruitful life seeking all those opportunities that had been shut out to me and my people. But now I knew this wasn't enough.

The final day of the retreat arrived, and with it the last meeting. At the conclusion of the evangelistic service an invitation was made to those present who wanted to accept Christ as Savior and Lord to come forward. For some reason I felt turned off. I hate being put on the spot for anything, and here I was being called on to make a public commitment, a statement of my intention to follow Jesus Christ. I hated public displays of emotion.

I saw people going forward and I revolted against the public appeal. This preacher, I said to myself, wants to manipulate people with guilt. I also felt that there was little intellectual integrity in people who could be coerced so easily into a decision that should affect them for the rest of their lives.

I left my seat, and I stepped out of the oppressive atmosphere of the meeting hall onto a busy street with crowded sidewalks and heavy traffic. Suddenly I felt totally alone, almost naked and transparent. I felt as if everybody around me was seeing all my little fears, doubts and problems. I felt very, very vulnerable.

As I hobbled along the street I wanted to evaporate, disappear, be lost forever in the crowd. I didn't understand, nor could I have guessed, that the Holy Spirit of God was holding a mirror up to myself.

As a thousand different thoughts rushed through my brain, I paused in mid-step and my head rang with the words of a song I recently heard: "If you are real, Lord, be real to me." This time I rewrote the lines and said to myself, "If the love of God is real, then let it be real to me." This was the acid test: could I really grow to love a people I deeply hated?

God's love was incredibly hard for me to understand. To comprehend the love of God in the face of my own suffering at the hands of people he made, and who were themselves taught from the Bible to love their neighbor—as long as he wasn't black—made no sense to me at all. Nevertheless, some part of me wanted to believe.

Quietly, almost as an act of desperation, I surrendered my life to God. I knew that Jesus Christ was the only way to have a relationship with God and I also knew that he would either be Lord of all or he would not be Lord at all. I had made a decision for life.

From now on I would take the Bible seriously as it applied to every area of my life, whatever the cost. In that decisive moment I knew my life would never be the same again. It would no longer be led by the uncontrolled passions of bitterness, rage and hatred, but by the ceaseless striving to love those I hated.

The traffic's din receded as I hobbled along the pavement and absorbed the night air. I felt a lightness in my heart that I had never felt before. My mind still swam with questions, yet somehow I felt reconciled within myself and to a God I could trust, who would control and order my life as never before.

After I made my commitment, I returned to the retreat center and talked to one of the leaders there. I felt it was necessary that I have basic answers to my questions about prayer, the faithfulness of God, and the trustworthiness of the Bible to carry me forward into an uncertain future.

A quiet exhilaration entered my soul, and the sheer joy of knowing I had made a decision climaxing months of doubt and uncertainty washed over me. Two Christian friends, one of whom had been with me from the beginning of my pilgrimage, prayed with me. His prayer was simple and he commended me to the love and service of God.

My initial discipleship began almost immediately. I was challenged by the American missionary and cofounder of Youth Alive, Mr. Allen Lutz, in my most vulnerable area—the need to love my enemy.

Despite my decision to take the Bible seriously, this challenge was a real struggle for me. I spent a lot of time studying and re-studying Jesus' words about loving enemies in the fifth chapter of Matthew's Gospel. My new mentor and I would talk for hours about what it meant to love my enemy. And I would tell him what I thought about white people and the situation in South Africa.

Allen Lutz was a great listener, and he was very understanding. His faith, like his life, was credible. Unlike other whites he came into our home, ate our food and experienced the inconveniences that came with living in Soweto. Even though we disagreed a lot of the time, I felt it was all right; he had earned the right to speak to me. He affirmed my faith and accepted the reality of my experience as a black man. I grew quickly in my faith.

My family could not understand my conversion. My mother, raised as a Lutheran, thought I was just ranting when I talked about a faith that was personal and intimate with a loving God who cared. Her textbook faith and learned formulas would not yield to my lively new-found expressions of joy and hope.

Over the years she had been very protective of me because of the accident that had left me crippled. She never agreed with my zealousness, but she never mocked me either. She remained supportive and even took my side at times when my brothers ridiculed me.

My father, on the other hand, simply waited for me to tire of the whole thing. However, as the weeks passed he became more and more impatient with me and my faith. He thought that the reality of Soweto's despair and hopelessness would drag me back to "reality." In his mind, my faith would soon collapse under its own weight.

The biggest test of my father's love came a year after I was converted.

It was the custom of African families to have the witch doctor come once a year to strengthen bonds between family members. This practice occurred among all tribal groups regardless of whether they had accepted the Christian religion or not.

Each family member formed a link in a chain and the function of the witch doctor was to strengthen the links. If any of the members did not participate in this ritual the linkages would be weakened and unfriendly spirits would invade the family. To refuse to participate in the ritual meant you did not love your family.

I was in a quandary. Of course I loved my family, but I loved Christ more. I owed him a higher allegiance. As a Christian, I could no longer participate in this ritual. My father, however, was adamant: undergo the ritual or leave the family home forever.

It became even more complicated for my father because the witch doctor had predicted that grave danger lay ahead for me. At first I tried to dismiss this as an attempt to manipulate me and my family. But knowing the reality of the forces of spiritual darkness, I could not take this prediction lightly. Neither could my father. The witch doctor wanted to ensure my safety with his spiritual powers, but I openly rejected his offer and assured my father that, if danger lay ahead, God would protect me.

I told my father that I understood his reasons for making me leave the family home. I knew he had no choice but to let me go. With sadness, I left.

It was almost three months to the day that the witch doctor's prediction came true—but with one difference. Just like the three Hebrew boys who were tossed into the fiery furnace during the reign of King Nebuchadnezzar but were not burned, God allowed me to be involved in a very serious car accident without injury.

The Youth Alive van that I was traveling in with several other young people rolled over three times when the driver failed to negotiate a sudden bend in a road. Five of the passengers were thrown out. I was trapped inside. When the van was righted I stepped out totally unharmed.

God showed himself sovereign in the accident. The fact

that I was unharmed forced my father to re-evaluate his attitude toward what I believed. He began to wonder if perhaps there was something to this Christian business after all. Without any preconditions he invited me to return home.

At home again, I received a better hearing from my brothers and sisters about my Christian faith. Some of them were curious enough to take an active interest in Christianity and to begin attending Sunday school.

My father and mother, now in their fifties, independently came to a living faith in Jesus Christ. This occurred when I was studying in the United States.

My father, who had stopped drinking when he was diagnosed as a severe diabetic, had begun to drink again. His drinking got out of hand and he went into a coma. Admitted to the hospital, he was given only a brief time to live. For days he hovered between life and death.

At one point he awoke to hear two nurses saying that he didn't have long to live. They didn't know he could hear them. In his semi-comatose state he prayed and asked God to heal him. Within four days he was out of the hospital.

He began to read the Bible and, very soon thereafter, gave his life to Christ. He stopped drinking and took his insulin regularly. His changed life profoundly affected my mother and she soon followed in his footsteps and committed her life to Jesus. They joined the local church where I was assistant pastor and later became founding members of Ebenezer Evangelical Church.

8

The Commission

The first real test of my faith came while I was still in high school. I had not yet spoken out about my faith or talked about what Jesus Christ meant to me.

It was the custom at school to have assembly every morning. At this time prayers and Scripture were read, and announcements were made by the principal.

In addition, a local preacher would be invited once a week to conduct a brief service. Some of the preachers who came were far less educated than we were. It was a great pastime for students to analyze what they said and to ridicule them if they made grammatical mistakes with their poor English. Our biology teacher used to have a field day exposing the "stupidity" of the Christian religion.

Because the principal was very positive toward Christianity and the reading of Scripture, he sometimes scheduled teaching staff to read the Bible when a preacher was not there. From time to time the biology teacher's turn would come around. He would stand up in front of the school and read the Bible as if it were the greatest book in the world. He did it to keep his job. In the classroom he spoke viciously against the Bible.

Every year the Gideon organization presented Bibles to first-year students. As a gesture of gratitude the principal would then arrange Bible readings every day for two weeks, and teachers would be assigned to make brief comments. Most of the teachers, including the biology teacher, merely went along with the whole exercise, exhibiting no real faith of their own. This so incensed some of us new Christians that we went to see the principal. We asked him if we could be given the opportunity to read the Scriptures. He agreed. Without argument the teachers stepped down in favor of the student Christians.

The next day, I was the first in line to read the Bible and talk briefly to 1,200 of my peers.

Some of the students gasped when they saw me go up to read; of all the students on campus I was the one thought least likely to volunteer for Bible reading. As I stood in front of the assembled body, I was trembling. The 1,200 students seemed like 12,000 as I looked out over a sea of faces, and my allotted five minutes seemed like five hours. I hadn't a clue how I would fill the time.

I read several verses, took a deep breath and began to speak. I told my schoolmates how I had almost been killed by a white man in an accident that crippled me for life. I had rejected Christianity because I saw it as the white man's religion. I went on to say that this was still a struggle inside me. Then I told them how I discovered the essential difference between organized religion and real faith: a personal encounter with Jesus Christ.

I briefly read another passage from the Bible and concluded my testimony by saying, "I don't really have much more to say about what I have read. But I can tell you that once I didn't understand passages like this, and now I do. Once I was blind, but now I see; once I was bound by sin, but now I'm free." I finished my speech and quietly stepped back into the audience.

The response by the students was overwhelming. More than fourteen students came to me and asked me to explain what had happened to my life. As a result, some of the students responded that day by committing their lives to Jesus Christ. Many are still staying with the commitment they made that day.

That was the first time I realized that my experience of faith could be talked about with and understood by others, and that people's lives could be changed by hearing about my faith.

The next day a small group of us began meeting during the lunch hour to discuss how we could apply our new-found faith to everyday life in Soweto. In a simple but direct way, faith in Christ became the driving, all-embracing force in our lives. It touched every aspect of our lives. It was not simply theoretical; it became intensely practical.

When several of us had no food the others shared what they had. When exam time came we banded together to study in the safest possible place, because the municipal police frequently raided our homes for rent the night before our exams. This happened so frequently in the homes of some of my Christian friends, that they would be psychologically handicapped before the exams. Many times failure had nothing to do with intelligence but with what happened the night before.

It has been documented that up until 1976 only five per cent of all the children who started school in Soweto would sit for the final matriculation exams in high school. The other ninety-five per cent would drop out of school at some point along the line. The whole system was stacked against the masses of black young people.

To pass secondary-school exams, we were tested in seven subjects. In addition to these subjects, we had to pass exams in three languages: English, Afrikaans and our mother tongue.

If we failed one of the three required languages, we failed everything. This meant that we had to repeat all the subjects, not just the one we failed. Another year would be lost. The fear of repeating the same class was so traumatic that it often resulted in students performing poorly. It was just as easy to fail a different subject the second time around. Often students who failed became disillusioned with the educational process and became permanent dropouts.

We Christians believed that our lives were in the hands of a caring God who understood our fears. This gave us great comfort and strength. We knew that, whether we passed or failed, our lives still had meaning and worth. God would never abandon us. And we also realized that the comfort our new-found faith offered had to be shared with our classmates.

One good strategy in sharing our faith was to take advantage of the work of the Gideons in their distribution of New Testaments in other schools. We formed a team and followed the Gideons from one school to the next. At each school, we invited the principal to set aside a week of morning assemblies to get students in the habit of reading the Bible. We would then volunteer to lead a couple of these assemblies.

In three months we went to every high school in Soweto. The result of these assemblies was seen in the swelling numbers of students who came to Youth Alive. Over the months I lost count of the number of converts we had from those morning assemblies.

It was during this time that my need to share the gospel with the thousands of young people caught up in the crushing cycles of educational failure, bitterness and anger was born. I began to sense a full-time call to preach and evangelize.

If I pursued this course my life, I knew, would never be the same. Ambitions for material success, education, good job, home, wife and children, money, the good life—such as it was in Soweto—could no longer hold the same appeal.

Up till now I was intent on doing law because all the black lawyers I knew were politically astute and had political power in the black community. Becoming a lawyer was a means of getting a good income and furthering my political ambitions, as well as being part of the future changes in my country. Becoming a Christian did not mean that I should not become a lawyer, but it did mean that I must put the kingdom of God first.

My desire to see justice done and righteousness imbedded in the heart of every man and woman made me increasingly angry at what I saw happening in a country dominated by a minority. My faith, as it grew and deepened, made me more sensitive to injustice.

70

I became frustrated with white people in South Africa who called themselves Christians. I was skeptical of any white person who claimed to be a Christian yet responded to the sinful state of South Africa with, "Well, what can I do?" I would say, "It is not a matter of what you can do. It's a matter of what you allow to go on in your presence or with your knowledge." I believed that many white people had a self-imposed powerlessness. It was to their advantage, after all, to maintain the status quo.

What I learned in those early years was that social justice, political freedom and Christianity are not mutually exclusive.

I now entered a period of uncertainty in my life. There were many directions I could go if I applied my mind and energies to seeking them out. Above all I wanted to do God's will and so I began to seek earnestly in prayer his direction for my life. I knew I could just as easily have gotten involved with agricultural missions and dealt with the abject poverty of the villages all around Johannesburg. Alternatively there lay the challenge of health care and social welfare. After my grim struggle to get my artificial leg and re-enter society as a disabled person, I saw a fulfilling vocation in providing counseling for others like myself who were going through adjustment problems in their lives.

But it was also during this time that I began to see the importance of dealing not only with the effects of human suffering, but with the underlying structures that caused the suffering in the first place.

I saw many people, including whites, who were quite willing to sacrifice time and money to alleviate the suffering of unemployed people, but who failed to confront the structural evil that created that unemployment. The way to deal with bad education for blacks was not to recruit well-meaning white teachers to help black students catch up with mathematics. Rather, we needed to get the government to scrap the Bantu Education Act and allocate equal resources to

71

all children regardless of their race, color or beliefs.

My involvement in Youth Alive convinced me more and more that whether evil structures produced evil people or evil people produced evil structures, people were the key to solving the underlying problems in my country.

In South Africa a white man staying scrupulously within the law can victimize a black man and feel no guilt. Yet, according to the Bible, that white man would be spiritually and morally accountable for the sin the structure allowed him to perpetuate. In South Africa a white landlord can legally refuse to rent an apartment to a black family, no matter how desperate that family's plight might be, because of the Group Areas Act. According to Jesus' teachings about love and justice, that white Christian landlord would need to disobey the act and provide housing for the family. Such a man would be radically following Jesus and not the status quo.

I yearned for that kind of change in my country. I knew that my future would involve a radical commitment to proclaiming Christ as Lord over all areas of life: personal, spiritual, political, economic and educational. Otherwise Jesus would not be Lord at all.

9

Going into Partnership

December 1969 was one of the most anxiety-filled months of my life. I was twenty years old and waiting for my matriculation results—results that could make or break me academically and thereby affect any future professional life I sought.

Everything hung on those exam results. I prayed, hoped and waited. As I did so, I was learning, in the midst of all the waiting, to trust God for my future. I spent several hours each day reading the Bible, praying and trying to discern what plans God had for my life.

One of the Bible passages that returned to me over and over again was Jesus' statement to his disciples about his church: "I will build my church and the gates of hell will not prevail against it."

This verse made a tremendous impression on me because of the direct manner in which Jesus asserted his divine intention. He was going to build a church that could withstand evil's full assault, and he was going to use ordinary people to build that church. There would be no celebrities—just twelve ordinary men plucked from everyday life to carry out the greatest mission in the history of the world.

Such people might easily have come from Soweto, the seething sprawl of humanity that was my home. Now, 2,000 years after Jesus lived on earth, I, a disenfranchised black living in a white-controlled and white-dominated society, wanted to be part of that unfolding drama. I felt a tremendous kinship with those early disciples. They were a small band of persecuted Jews living under a cruel, repressive Roman government. It was not unlike the oppressive apartheid government of South Africa that I and my people were living under.

It was a great relief to both me and my parents when the letter arrived from the Department of Bantu Education informing them that I had passed my exams. I was eligible to enter the university.

What I saw now so clearly in South Africa was a white church that was in league with the political philosophy of apartheid and collaborating in the oppression of blacks. I also saw the black church as irrelevant and isolationist.

The church that Jesus intended to build was, from all human appearances, made up of weak and downtrodden people with no academic, political or economic power. And yet those weak and downtrodden disciples were the ones to whom the keys of the kingdom of heaven were given and through whom mighty empires would be challenged. It was not a weak and ineffective church that Jesus envisaged but rather a dynamic and vibrant force that dared to go boldly into the very strongholds of oppressive political forces and prevail.

As I thought about the uncertainties of my life, I drew consolation from knowing that I was part of the church that Jesus had been building for the past 2,000 years. The question arose in my own mind: how could I be involved in the same way as those seemingly unqualified men were so long ago? God was still God, wasn't he? He was not caught in some time warp. He was still in the business of building his church. But could I be a part of it?

In asking the question, I answered it. I knew I desperately wanted to be part of God's plan. I refused to believe that the image of the church as a holding operation—snatching a few souls from the abyss till the final curtain was drawn—was an accurate picture of what Jesus was talking about. There was a dynamic in Jesus' teaching that demanded I be in the "construction business" of building his kingdom. I looked forward with eager anticipation to the plan God would show me for my life's work.

One of the greatest obstacles however, to a yes answer to this question was the position my father took about the possibility of my ever being a minister of religion. He was very cautious about my new-found faith and he opposed the black clergy in Soweto who were largely uneducated, weak men—men who had sold out to white missionaries for their financial support. He tried to extract a promise from me that I would not consider being a minister.

Even though I did not promise him that I would not be a minister, I knew what he would say if I abandoned pursuing a legal career. It was not a decision I could or would take lightly. I wanted his love and approval, but I knew that they could not come at any cost.

It was during this period that Youth Alive leaders challenged me to consider spending one year, before going to the university, as part of a team of four men that would travel throughout South Africa, preaching the gospel and sharing our faith. Diamond Atong was one of the team members. I saw this as an opportunity to expose myself to actual ministry situations that would help me to evaluate my call to the full-time ministry.

Our program was so successful in school assemblies and public rallies that we received invitations to present the program in England and the United States.

Before leaving on our overseas tour, we traveled extensively throughout southern Africa, Botswana and Swaziland. This trip was marked by the death of one of my closest friends on the team. His name was Jerome Tunce, and he died of tuberculosis.

Jerome's death was the tragic result of the government's health-care system for blacks, with few doctors, poor facilities and aging equipment. By the time his tuberculosis was finally diagnosed, Jerome had already been to three doctors. The first doctor gave Jerome lozenges for his persistent cough. The second doctor said he had a chronic chest infection, but he could take no x-rays. A third doctor said he had gastroenteritis. Finally, a doctor in a Presbyterian hospital in Swaziland diagnosed Jerome with tuberculosis. He was immediately quarantined. But it was too late. Jerome died two days later.

Jerome's death affected us all deeply. I was his closest friend, and his death shattered me. I wondered if I could continue the tour. A young man who had committed his life to Christ was dead. For the first time since I became a Christian I seriously questioned God's love and wisdom. In my mind it seemed a terrible loss to our ministry and to God's work in the world. Jerome was capable of doing so much more with his life than many Christians I knew. Why, if God cared so much, did he allow Jerome's life to be cut short? Why couldn't God have intervened to save him?

I was shaken by Jerome's death, but I was even more disturbed by God's apparent silence. The mystery of suffering would remain just that. I had experienced much suffering myself and was seeing God's redemptive hand in it. But it seemed that Jerome's death was both premature and meaningless. After considerable prayer I finally resigned myself to the fact that there were simply some things my finite mind could not comprehend and for which there were no simple answers. I was comforted with the thought that Jerome was now with Jesus in heaven, but a part of me longed for his friendship here on earth. His death forced me to reflect more deeply on the cross of Christ and on what it cost God to allow his own son to die for our sins.

Life would go on, but I would miss Jerome deeply.

The trip to the United States and Europe proved to be both spiritually and emotionally challenging. It opened our eyes to the reality that had shaped the lives of many missionaries to our land. We had a better understanding of their attitudes toward us and of why many of them were so poorly informed about life in an African context of racial conflict, poverty and suffering.

I discovered that it was easy for many of my overseas friends to divorce their Christian faith from the social context in which they lived.

A good example of the differences between us came when we talked about racial justice. For us it was a matter of upholding God's standards of justice and righteousness as they are reflected in the Bible. For Americans—even American Christians—racism merely violated a constitutional right.

We also discovered that, because of our experiences of suffering, our faith bore a deeper dimension. When we prayed, "Give us this day our daily bread," it was meant quite literally. Our European and North American friends simply had no comprehension of this. These discoveries made the trip both challenging and exhausting.

We found a high level of interest among our white friends in the West but also a lot of ignorance. We were forced to educate them about the black struggle.

Likewise, many of our supporting churches never had the opportunity to hear black Africans talk about the racial divisions within South Africa. Everything those churches knew had been taught to them by whites. Therefore, most of them had the impression that the white South African government was good to black people and that the problems in South Africa were caused by Communist agitators. This played into the fears of many Western Christians who genuinely believed that the Third World was caving in to Communism.

The truth was that we were open to the gospel that white missionaries presented, but their gospel was devoid of cultural sensitivity and failed to speak to our social condition. Their gospel endorsed the racial status quo and failed to challenge the social and political sin of apartheid. The missionaries wanted to save our souls for heaven, but they forgot we had bodies on earth.

Despite the challenge of the trip, there were also some hilarious moments. On one occasion, a young white boy in a small Pennsylvania town woke up to find a "chocolate-covered" man sleeping on the living-room sofa. He rushed to his mother in shock, shouting, "Mother, there's a man on the couch covered in chocolate sauce! Why doesn't he wash it off?" The boy came over to me and tried to rub it off. I laughed uproariously. The incident, however, reflected some of the isolation we noticed among many white Christians in North America. But we never allowed these awkward moments to develop negative attitudes in us. Our hosts were loving and concerned for our spiritual welfare.

In those three months we traveled extensively, preaching and singing wherever we went. The commitment to missions in most of these churches was heartwarming. In some churches, we met people who prayed for us daily and who knew us very well. I began to understand why at times our efforts were fruitful in spite of our often inadequate preparation. To this day I am thankful for believers everywhere who pledged themselves to pray for us and our ministry regularly.

In the end, we made many friends as we traveled through the United States, Canada and England. Many of them still support our work today.

During my travels I was challenged by the spiritual need that I saw in young people everywhere. Many were hostile to the church because of its insensitivity toward and lack of understanding for the problems of black youth. Many of these young people had legitimate grievances against the church and organized religion that needed answers. Their hurt and pain, their questions and searchings, needed a response. I wanted to be a part of their search for answers. I wanted them to know Jesus Christ as I did, as a Savior who could liberate them from the power of sin and help them to accept who they were.

I saw during this time that the Youth Alive method of getting young people to share their faith with their peers was an effective form of evangelism. I also recognized that it was going to take a total commitment on the part of Youth Alive to reach young people for Christ while at the same time raising the conscience of the church to its responsibility for young people. For the first time I began to think about the need for genuine partnerships between those missionary-sending countries, with their traditional mission agencies, and the mission fields they served.

It was also during this trip to the United States that I met Mr. Bob Nanfelt, a New Jersey businessman who had almost lost his leg in a carpentry accident. In gratitude to God for saving his leg, he started a fund for missions.

At Brookdale Baptist Church in Bloomfield, New Jersey, he heard our presentation about Youth Alive. After the service we discussed using his fund to help Third World students attend Bible college for training.

I had not as yet articulated what I felt God wanted me to do, but I realized that this meeting might be God's way of telling me what he wanted for my life. I agreed to be the first recipient of Bob Nanfelt's fund. We looked through several college catalogs together. One of the colleges that stood out was Northeastern Bible College in Essex Fells, New Jersey, just a short drive from where we were.

Northeastern's proximity to New York City, where a large segment of black South Africans lived as exiles, encouraged me to study there. The possibility of contact with fellow countrymen would ease my occasional homesickness, and interacting with these political exiles would help me to focus my studies more directly on the South African situation. Northeastern was the perfect choice.

Yet I was not under pressure to decide immediately. This gave me the opportunity to go back home to Soweto to talk to my parents and assess the situation before making a final commitment.

I knew that in the United States my life would be a thousand times easier and that I would enjoy enormous democratic freedoms. But as glamorous as studying in the United States sounded, I was realistic enough to know that I would have major adjustment problems too. I needed time to weigh the pros and cons of being temporarily separated from my own culture while adjusting to life in America. I also knew there would be a period of readjustment back into South African life once my studies ended. In addition, I was going to study the Christian faith in a context that was totally foreign to my own; would I be able to return to South Africa and step back into a world of people who knew nothing but oppression?

After receiving counsel from the Youth Alive leaders who were traveling with us from Soweto, it seemed right that I return to South Africa for at least six months to gain additional ministry experience before Bible college. I returned to South Africa with the team.

From January to June of 1971 I worked as volunteer staff with Youth Alive in Soweto. During this time I had an itinerant ministry among the high schools of Soweto. I got to know the problems of black education more deeply and felt that my call to full-time youth work was confirmed.

It was also during this time that I was introduced to a young woman who was to change my life in new and different ways. She knew of my ministry but we had never met. Her name was Nomchumane Nyangiwe or "Chumi." She was a student nurse.

We barely had time to get to know each other before I left for the United States.

10
Marriage and Missions

I spent the next four years at Northeastern Bible College in Essex Fells, New Jersey, studying the Bible and living among other international students in a multicultural setting. This gave me an opportunity to evaluate my faith and put deeper roots into my evangelical heritage.

At the same time, my relationship with Chumi—carried out entirely by mail—was deepening. I now realized that I loved her and could not imagine the rest of my life without her. Marriage seemed inevitable, but the long-distance courtship posed a challenge. My love for Chumi and hers for me had grown and developed entirely by correspondence. We both wrote each other numerous poems during this time. The ten thousand miles which separated us as I studied in the United States and she pursued her nursing career in Soweto seemed like a million miles. There were times when I simply wanted to leap across the waters to be with her to share my life and future with her. Practicing patience was difficult.

Marriage plans by correspondence were complicated enough. To further complicate matters, tradition demanded that I convince my uncles to ask her parents for her hand in marriage. This would have to wait until I returned to South Africa.

I spent many hours washing dishes at the Bible college during that year to earn enough money for the trip. When the last dollar had been earned and the plane ticket bought, all I could think about was Chumi and the life I hoped, by God's grace, to share with her. I finally returned to South Africa in

May 1974.

It took a week of evening discussions with my uncles to convince them that I was ready to get married. The difficulty for them was that my bank balance did not give them enough confidence to approach Chumi's parents. My uncles knew that they would have to prove I would be able to take care of Chumi. And my uncles did not share our faith that God would see us through the good times and bad—with or without money.

My father, relieved that I had decided not to marry a foreigner while in the States, took it upon himself to persuade the others to support the marriage proposal. My father did not know that it was out of the question for me to consider marrying a foreigner. A foreigner could not have settled happily in the political context of South Africa. Also, my three years in the United States had changed me. I knew that when I returned for good to South Africa, I would need Chumi to help me make the transition.

Within three months I had the support of all the family members from both sides. At that point Chumi and I got engaged. I bought her a ring in Johannesburg and invited all of our friends from Youth Alive and our local church for an engagement party at her home.

Because of my school schedule, I returned to the United States and college in August of that year to await Chumi's arrival. The wait seemed like an eternity compared to the three-year correspondence we had had across the Atlantic.

It was wonderful to see Chumi finally burst through the immigration doors at Kennedy Airport after her hilarious experience trying to explain to the customs officials how she was hoping to live with a husband who washed dishes at a Bible college. It took an hour of negotiations between Chumi, who spoke English with a black South African accent, and an American customs official, who spoke English with a Bronx accent, before the customs officials realized her husband-to-be was actually a foreign student with full financial support, not merely a dishwasher.

Chumi and I were married May 18, 1975. It was her birthday and the day after my graduation from Northeastern.

One of the highlights of the wedding was the presence of Chumi's uncle, who had been in exile in New York since 1960. He brought a number of friends with him, and they sang African songs to the delight of our American guests who had never heard that kind of singing before.

Chumi's uncle was one of thousands of exiles forced to leave South Africa when the African National Congress was banned and it looked certain that all political activists would land in jail. He settled in New York and married a woman from South Africa.

Two weeks after our wedding we drove our 1964 Chevy Impala from Essex Fells, New Jersey, to Wheaton, Illinois, to begin the next phase of our life together. I had been given a two-year scholarship to study communications at the graduate school of Wheaton College, a leading and highly respected Christian institution of higher learning.

Chumi and I arrived on a hot, humid day in July and were welcomed by a group of African students. With their assistance we adjusted quickly into graduate-school life. Our relationships with these students opened up a whole new way of thinking about missions in southern Africa.

Up to this point we had experienced missions as essentially white dominated, controlled by foreign missionaries with the approval of the South African government. The mission agencies in South Africa were impenetrable to black leadership. This, in effect, kept the African in a second-class position within the churches that the missionaries established.

Our discussions at Wheaton frequently centered on this problem: if missions were to be dominated by whites from the West, should we have a moratorium on foreign missionaries going to Africa?

The first black African to suggest this openly was the Rev. John Gatu, a student at Wheaton at the time and later an evangelical church leader in East Africa. He argued that there needed to be a breathing space for Africans to form their own mission groups and evangelize their own people without outside interference. He had grown increasingly concerned with how the gospel was constantly wrapped in Western cultural trappings.

Another of the Wheaton group of African students, Mr. Pius Wakatama, from what was then Rhodesia (now Zimbabwe), challenged us with the call to independence from foreign missions in order to allow black churches and their leaders to emerge and for African churches to be self-determining. While he did not advocate a moratorium on Western missionaries to Africa, he opposed what he called "missionary colonialism." He stressed the need for a New Testament approach, pointing out that the apostles visited a new place for a few months to evangelize and establish a church and then left for other unreached areas. The apostle Paul gave his instructions and exhortations through letters, by messengers or on return visits; he never settled down in one place for years.

Mr. Wakatama's perspectives challenged me to critically re-evaluate the reasons for the lack of growth of mission churches and the dearth of black national leadership in South Africa. Western missionaries came to our country, established their mission stations, and stayed beyond their usefulness, accepting the reigning political philosophy of apartheid without challenging its inherent evil.

My studies at Wheaton under such notable men as Dr. James Engel, Dr. Vic Oliver and Dean Norton helped me to apply the social sciences to evangelism.

I also began to see history and theology in a new light. Some saw history as neatly boxed into certain time periods or compartments. This view of history also boxed God in as to how he should act in our own day. By restricting the acts of God to limited periods of history, many Christians were able to dispense with certain portions of the Bible as no longer relevant for today. God, I realized, would not be so contained in man-made boxes. Jesus' Sermon on the Mount is as relevant today as it was when Jesus said it 2,000 years ago.

My studies at Wheaton College helped me to ask critical questions about how missions could be practiced in the coming decades. With the support of experienced African thinking on missions, I was able, during this time, to explore helpful avenues of partnership with churches in the West.

In 1976, after two years of study, I graduated with my Masters degree. Chumi and I made plans to spend the next three months in the United States encouraging people to commit themselves to pray for and financially support Youth Alive in Soweto. Enlisting the prayers of friends was very important to us. We were convinced then, as we are now, that it takes more than money to have a fruitful ministry.

Within two days of my graduation, however, our plans changed. Political events in South Africa were unfolding in ways we never could have predicted. On June 16, 1976, thirteen-year-old Hector Petersen was shot and killed during a school demonstration in the streets of Soweto.

11

Hector Petersen and After

Everyone in Soweto knows the name of Hector Petersen. He was a thirteen-year-old schoolboy who joined a protest march on June 16, 1976, and was shot dead by riot police.

Hector was participating in a protest march against the use of Afrikaans as the teaching language for subjects like science and mathematics in Bantu schools. The protest represented the biggest threat to white security since the shootings in Sharpeville.

Black students were saying, "You'll push us no further." This flew in the face of the Afrikaner understanding of the "happy natives" who should appreciate all that the whites were doing for them.

There were 20,000 other schoolchildren marching in the streets of Soweto that day. After those fateful twenty-four hours, seven schoolchildren had died, two whites had been lynched, police dogs had been knifed and set alight, and the offices of the Department of Bantu Administration Board had been destroyed.

Hector Petersen's death, the first of what would be so many, marked the beginning of a new era of confrontation. White security would never be the same. The riots set off a chain reaction around the country and, finally, around the world. Within four months of June 16, 1976, 160 black communities had vented their fury.

Overnight, Soweto—that dust-filled urban sprawl which I called my home—became famous. Chumi and I looked on from America and wept for Hector Petersen. The sight on an

American television screen of a black boy running along a Soweto street holding Hector Petersen's lifeless body jolted Chumi and me into the realization that we had to return immediately and stand with our suffering brothers and sisters.

We packed our few belongings and said goodbye to our friends. Tears mingled with prayers as we stood in a circle and prayed together. We knew we would probably never see each other again.

We left Wheaton a few days after graduation and flew back to Johannesburg and Youth Alive, not knowing what we would find or which of our friends had been killed or detained. The wreckage of government buildings, the road-blocks and the rows of cheap coffins were some of the sights greeting us during those first few days back in Soweto.

We realized that the dehumanization caused by apartheid was now coming full circle. The value of human life had completely disappeared for many people: blacks and whites both were seeing each other as symbols that could be destroyed without regard for personalities, families, homes or backgrounds. People had become disposable units for the trash can. One soldier who came out of Soweto boasted the highest number of bullets discharged in the shortest period of time. These were bullets fired not at some powerful army coming to invade his country, but at unarmed men, women and children who were born in his own land.

On the other side, there was the tragic irony of the first white man to be killed. Dr. Melville Leonard Edelstein, a Jewish sociologist who worked in Soweto and might have been sympathetic to the social and political needs of black people, was killed on June 16. Edelstein's work in Soweto was no safeguard against black rage. Trust had been eroded.

What followed was one shock after another, polarizing black and white communities. The cry for law and order by the white community resulted in the occupation of black townships by South African defense forces. Road blocks and humiliating searches by the army were carried out randomly.

Black leaders and their followers went into exile. Families lived anxiously from day to day. Panic ensued each time a person did not come home at the expected time; often families would visit mortuaries, police stations and hospitals wondering what could have happened to their loved ones. It was a daily struggle not to be crushed by the iron fist of military occupation or to give way to bitterness.

There were 176 deaths in the first week, and funerals were held on most weekends. The government was afraid of the huge crowds, and for a while banned all weekend funerals and mass meetings and placed restrictions on the funerals that were allowed.

Black people refused to obey the restrictions. The numbers attending the funerals showed the extent to which the black voice had been suppressed. In response, every funeral was attended by large numbers of police and army in camouflage uniforms. At the slightest hint of a political speech, they would order the crowd to disperse. Each funeral saw more people being shot; from that, more funerals occurred.

I was at one such funeral in Doornkop, Soweto. There was a crowd of about 7,000 thronging the grave of a young man who had died in detention from internal bleeding, a victim of the police brutality that occurs during interrogation. The people were singing freedom songs when the police arrived in huge army trucks which they parked just outside the fence, dividing the graveyard from the rest of the township.

A policeman stepped forward and in his normal voice—without a megaphone—shouted for the boy's father. He said he wanted the father of the boy to tell the people to go. He called: "I want the father! Where is the father?"

The fringe of the crowd began to get agitated and some of them picked up stones. Several newspaper reporters told the people, "Please be calm. Don't throw any stones." They knew that if the police opened fire there would be a massacre. The policeman called again, "Where is the father?" But there was no way the father could have heard in a crowd of 7,000.

89

Finally, the officer shouted at us to disperse. He said it three times: "Disperse or we will open fire." It seemed like a bad dream. On the third "disperse" they began shooting.

To this day I cannot remember how I got out of that place without being shot. As they opened fire, I turned to Chumi and said, "Run." Our safest bet was to get into a stationary car and sit there. I thought they wouldn't shoot at a stationary vehicle. But at that moment my father, who had been standing next to me all along, suddenly went limp and fell against me. I half-dragged, half-carried him to the minibus. There was nothing else I could do—I simply had to keep walking despite the gunfire all around us. I said to him, "If they shoot us, that's it."

It seemed like an eternity before we reached the car. When we did, Chumi was not to be found. I looked over my shoulder and saw that she had fallen in the rush to flee the flying bullets. I was certain she had been shot and killed. I went back to pick her up. Though she lay very still, she was unharmed. Her dress was ripped and she had lost her watch and shoes.

We climbed into the minibus. At the same moment a car next to us, a British-made Triumph, took off at high speed. A policeman shouted, "There go the leaders!" Immediately they opened fire and everyone in the car was killed. They sprayed the car with bullets, ripping the whole vehicle to pieces.

We waited till everything had quieted down and then I got out of the car. I asked one of the policemen if I could take some of the injured to a hospital.

"No," he said.

"Please," I said. "These people are going to bleed to death."

"No," he repeated, more vehemently this time. Then, suddenly, he changed his mind. "All right. If you want your car to get bloodied, you can take them." We took about fifteen injured to Baragwanath Hospital.

When we got to the hospital the orderlies who opened the

back of the minibus told us that three of our passengers were already dead. At the hospital we found a number of newspaper reporters hanging around, and I was interviewed at length by a reporter from the *Star,* a liberal white-owned newspaper. When we got back home later in the afternoon, I opened the minibus doors and took photographs of the blood on the floor. All that week I couldn't sleep. I kept thinking of the horror I had seen that day.

After consulting with other church leaders I decided to make a tape recording for the minister of police. I described what had happened in detail. I told him that it was unnecessary to open fire on people who were unarmed and that the only way to prevent a repetition of such terrible carnage was to disarm the riot police. If they must have weapons, I said, let them use tear gas, with plastic shields to block any thrown stones. I was speaking out of a deep Christian conviction that what was going on was wrong. It had been a massacre of the innocents and I felt that, even if funerals were banned, what happened that day would only fan the violence. Eventually the tape was returned to me and the message was clear: "Don't raise any dust. If you do, some of the junior officers might do something irrational." It was a thinly veiled threat telling me to keep my mouth shut.

My earlier interview with the *Star* was published. The story had been edited so severely I was unable to recognize the account of the facts I had given the reporter. Obviously there had been severe censorship by the editors.

I couldn't believe what was happening to us in South Africa. I realized how ordinary, peace-loving people could be radicalized. Those who believed in gradual and nonviolent solutions to South Africa's problems found themselves hard pressed to justify their position. They eventually learned to live with violence, seeing that, perhaps, it was the only language the oppressors understood.

Everyone was affected by the brush of violence. Hardly a family remained untouched in one way or another, and everyone wanted retribution. I felt so angry and wounded,

I could have picked up a machine gun myself and shot all the whites around me. As it happened, I came very close to killing a man a few days after the funeral massacre.

Another protest march had been organized to demonstrate against the government. Unaware of the march, I was driving the Youth Alive minibus through the area. As I rounded a corner I saw a large crowd of about 300 students marching toward Orlando West High School. Parked across the street, in the path of the march, was a police car. Balancing a rifle on the roof of the car was a white policeman whom I had heard much about. He was notoriously trigger-happy. It was obvious to me that he was going to shoot into the crowd of students. In a second I could have driven into him with the minibus, killing him instantly. I wanted to do it. I was angry enough and felt justified enough to slam the accelerator pedal to the floor.

Chumi was sitting next to me and she knew what I was thinking. Instinctively she said, "No," and I slammed on the brakes. The policeman immediately saw us. Looking at my face he saw the anger and in an instant realized I could have used the minibus as a weapon to kill him. Without a word he jumped into his car and sped away.

Seeing that man so ready to kill defenseless schoolchildren made me angry and bitter. If I had not possessed a strong faith, bitterness like that could have overtaken me. In truth, it's still the one thing I fear the most. I have to pray daily and say at such moments, "God, please save me today from bitterness. Save me today from irrational hatred. Let me be angry, let me be absolutely disgusted, let me feel the worst contempt for my situation, but save me from bitterness." When you become bitter, you become irrational, and then you act irrationally. Sometimes I am asked how long I can hold out against the bitterness, and sometimes I wonder myself. But in the end, rather than go the way of a bitter heart, I would leave this country—the land of my birth—because I know that once I become bitter I will become useless to God and to my own people.

12
Student Turmoil

> *Because the white missionary described black people as thieves, lazy, sex-hungry etc., and because he equated all that was valuable with whiteness, our Churches through our ministers see all these vices I have mentioned above not as manifestations of the cruelty and injustice which we are subjected to by the white man but inevitable proof that after all the white man was right when he described us as savages. Thus if Christianity in its introduction was corrupted by the inclusion of aspects which made it the ideal religion for the colonization of people, nowadays in its interpretation it is the ideal religion for the maintenance of the subjugation of the same people.*

Steve Biko, *"The Church As Seen by a Young Layman"*

During my theological studies in the United States, I was forced to come to terms with the words and thoughts of Steve Biko, a young South African leader in the Black Consciousness Movement. There were a number of black leaders during that time who radically influenced my thinking about religion and spirituality as they related to black experience. Many of these leaders paid for their beliefs with their lives, and their movements were banned by the South African government in the late 1970s.

Biko taught that religion was useless unless it also taught people that oppression is a sin. It was important, he said, not to acquiesce or cooperate in one's own oppression nor to stand idly by and watch one's brothers and sisters being oppressed. Men like Barney Pitjana, an Anglican clergyman, put into words the theological implications of the Black Consciousness philosophy which Biko espoused. I knew that my evangelical tradition would have to respond clearly to the crisis in South Africa—and soon.

An opportunity for response came much sooner than I had anticipated. In 1974 I was invited to speak to the Student Christian Movement (SCM) conference of evangelical students in South Africa. The annual conference was being held at Moriya in Lesotho at a facility owned by the Roman Catholic church.

The SCM was a breakaway organization from the Student Christian Association, one of the most effective Christian student movements of its time. Even before 1965, SCA was racially integrated, incorporating all students. However, a student leader named Andries Treuernicht decided that it was not good for black, white, Indian and coloured to belong to the same organization. His actions brought about a split in the SCA, resulting in separate student movements for Afrikaners, blacks, coloureds, Indians and English-speaking whites. Thus the SCM, a black student movement, was born.

The 1974 conference was attended by several men who would later become prominent leaders of the black struggle for political rights in South Africa, including Cyril Ramaphosa, general secretary of the National Union of Mineworkers; Lybon Mabaso, the founder and president of the Azanian Peoples Organization; Griffiths Zabala, of Self-Help and Development Economics; and Frank Chikane, general secretary of the Institute for Contextual Theology and, later, general secretary of the South African Council of Churches.

The conference was completely run by students, since the organizers could not afford the luxury of paid workers. This made it possible for students to develop a program that spoke directly to the heated issues raised by the Black Consciousness movements on their campuses.

It was here that Steve Biko's speeches and writings influenced what a Christian posture ought to be for black university students. Given the volatile racial tension that had resulted in the birth of the SCM, discussions on the relationship between black and white Christians were very explosive.

My duty at the conference was to lead discussions and Bible studies on the implications of the gospel for issues such as Black Consciousness, the use of violence in the struggle for liberation and the difficult task of reconciliation.

Reconciliation was a major concern. Not only had we evangelical Christians separated ourselves into racial splinter groups, but we were divided even within the SCM on the issue of how best to challenge the inhumanity of apartheid. Our lack of unity became painfully evident twenty-four hours into the SCM conference, when we had to resolve a potentially violent situation.

A government informer from the Black University of Fort Hare was discovered among those in attendance. His presence touched a raw nerve in everyone present, splitting the crowd into two angry groups. Some at the conference actually wanted him killed. Others argued that this was not an option for people who call themselves Christians.

Before we could resolve what should be done, we had to bring the two factions together. We spent most of that evening calming the student body so that the leadership could conduct the discussions in an orderly manner. We sat precariously on the edge of a crisis.

As a black leader I was asked to respond first to the crisis. I desperately wanted justice to be done; at the same time I did not want to be responsible for a lynching. I prayed hard, asking God to give me the wisdom to know what to say and, above all, how to say it. I wanted to be faithful to Scripture in my speech, knowing that a man's life hung in the balance.

When my moment came I stood before the assembled crowd and asked for their silence. I opened my Bible to the passage in the Gospel of John that speaks about Christ's death. For the next twenty minutes I spoke on the way of the cross. I told them of Christ's vulnerability in the face of his own betrayal and his willingness to die for what he believed was true, in obedience to his father's will. Since we passionately believed that what we stood for at that conference was truth, it really didn't matter what was reported by any informer. Apartheid would have the last word unless our generation accepted suffering and even betrayal for what we believed were God's standards of justice and righteousness. We had to bear our cross faithfully. In doing so, we would enter into the fellowship of the sufferings of Christ.

I said that violence always leads to greater violence; once you start down that slippery slope, you cannot be stopped easily. If we chose vengeance and retribution, many people would die in the ensuing violence.

At the end of my speech I sat down, fearful of the consequences but knowing in my heart that what I said was right. Only God could now vindicate me.

The assembled crowd stood and applauded. I felt a strange sense of elation. A great calm came over me. Life had triumphed over death. The informer would live. But he had been publicly shamed, and he soon left the conference.

There were other serious issues regarding violence that we wanted to resolve that evening but couldn't. We were all too emotionally drained by what had happened. We wanted to resolve how to legitimately defend the helpless and powerless and determine what we should do and how we should act in the face of victimization. For the moment, however, we resolved not to use violence.

The chasms that separated evangelical Christians only mirrored the deeper divisions found in the broader South African context, and my heart ached for the reconciliation I knew was available to us if we simply believed and followed the gospel of Jesus Christ.

Jesus' prayer for unity among his followers was now my fervent prayer. I yearned for it. True reconciliation would never be brought about by violence. The political order could never change men's hearts. Only the transforming power of the Holy Spirit could change South Africa.

13

The ANC Option
and Imprisonment

My brother George is a very intelligent man, the fourth of
seven brothers in our family. More than anything else he
dreamed of being a journalist. But his dreams were never to
be realized. Any employment he undertook never quite got
off the ground. He was always frustrated by the oppressive
policies of apartheid that even affected the workplace.
Eventually he realized that even if he had become a journalist, government restrictions would never allow him to meet
his own high ideals of truth and accuracy in reporting.

During the mid-1970s, newspaper editors were white and
editorial policies reflected their bias toward the government's racial stance. Furthermore, blacks had none of the
resources to create an alternative press. It was therefore not
necessary for the government to have stringent censorship;
the white community, in whose interest apartheid was being
upheld, maintained full control.

In the early 80s, world pressure on the apartheid government of Prime Minister Botha began to have an effect, and
alternative media arose in South Africa. The government
could no longer rely on the unsolicited support of the white
press; what was happening in the country was too explosive to
be covered up—even by the white press. On top of this, the
black community began having more and more access to
overseas publications. When the overseas media publicized
major events—especially conflict within the country—they

often contradicted the South African government and the pro-government press.

The truth about riots, police brutality, restrictions, the banning of publications and unrelenting political activism could not be hidden unless the government acted decisively. This it did. The government made it illegal for any journalists residing in South Africa to report on or publish news related to national security—either in South African papers or abroad—without police clearance.

These measures were so restrictive that they forced many journalists to rise up in protest. News reporters formed unions and demanded their right to publish what they saw as the truth.

The *Rand Daily Mail,* a liberal white newspaper, tried unsuccessfully to incorporate the demands of the new unions. Even though it enjoyed a large circulation among educated blacks, the white readership soon dropped so drastically that the paper was forced to cease publication. This was a tragedy, but it mirrored the deep hostility many whites felt toward blacks in general. That they were able to force a newspaper to go out of business by boycotting it both in advertising and sales showed the enormous power of the white-controlled economy.

Each time a "state of emergency" was declared in the country, newspaper reporting was the first to suffer government suppression. The severest suppression came in 1986 when the government actually put the onus on publishers to censor themselves or else fall under the iron fist of the Censorship Board.

My brother George was caught up in the early stages of the struggle for press freedom. In the mid-70s he worked for a brief period as a newspaper photographer, traveling with one of South Africa's best-known journalists, Doc Bikitsha. But George could not survive under the heavy press restrictions, so he gave up his ambition to be a journalist. The government would not let him report the real issues of the day, which had to do with the pain of his people's subjugation. His heart ached for his people, and he longed to write about the agony in his soul and the souls of his people. But the endless stream of restrictions boxed him into a corner from which he could not move. For two years George went through utter misery as he moved from one job to the next, unhappy at anything he did. The reason was always the same: he could not stand the superior attitude of his white employers.

During 1977, while I was wrestling with the deep truths of Scripture and learning to relate God's standards of justice and righteousness to black South Africa, my brother saw the violent overthrow of the white government as the only way forward for himself.

That year, he obtained employment as a truck driver, delivering nationalist magazines for an Afrikaans publishing company in Johannesburg. With access to this truck, he was able to shuttle African National Congress recruits between Johannesburg and the Botswana border. Most of these recruits were teens who had been involved in riots, and their activities had brought them into confrontation with the police. Rather than face detention, torture and eventual imprisonment, they chose to leave the country illegally. This was a very dangerous thing both for the recruits and for those who were helping them.

George cleverly duped the white soldiers manning the road blocks by offering them a free magazine from his clearly marked delivery truck. As a result, they let him pass into Botswana without a vehicle check. My brother was very careful not to talk about these escapades. Danger lurked at every turn of the road. The drivers could never be sure when or where the next patrol or road block would be. They were exposed to the possibility of capture every time they saw a soldier or were forced to stop for inspection. During these trips, George would often have as many as fifteen ANC recruits hidden under piles of magazines in the back of his truck.

After several months of successfully ferrying recruits into Botswana he was forced to resign: his activities had become known to the security forces of the South African government.

Two months earlier a journalist friend of his, Aicken Ramudzuli, was arrested, and George's clandestine ANC activities were extracted from him during sustained periods of torture. Ramudzuli's revelations led to investigations which resulted in the death of Nicholas, a schoolteacher in Soweto and one of George's friends. Nicholas was a key political activist in the ANC who had extensive knowledge of the recruitment networks. When the police came to arrest him, Nicholas resisted. He died in a shootout in his Soweto room, but not before he killed several police in the process.

Before his death Nicholas sent a warning to George, who was at that time traveling somewhere between Johannesburg and the Botswana border. The message was: "Don't return. Get out immediately. Everything is known about our activities." Incredibly George got the message. That same night, with all hope of making a significant contribution to black politics now gone, he fled across the border into Botswana. He became both an ANC refugee himself and a permanent exile from his beloved country.

In Botswana he officially joined the ANC and was trained in methods of organizing underground cells and in sabotage. He was put in charge of developing ANC underground networks in the Witwaterstrand region, and he made periodic excursions into South Africa from Swaziland.

The first time I knew George was coming and going out of the country was when the car carrying me and other members of the Youth Alive executive committee was held up in a road block about thirty kilometers from the Swaziland border. The security forces recognized my surname on the passbook. They suspected that I either had contact with George or was one of the channels that the liberation movement used.

With me were Cyril Ramaphosa, chairman of the board of Youth Alive and an up-and-coming young lawyer who had defended many trade-union cases, and Phillip Nkabinde, a school principal and general secretary of the Alliance church, a denomination doing extensive work in Mozambique. Our presence raised the level of suspicion of the security forces. They radioed for reinforcements because they thought we posed a threat too big for them to handle.

What followed were several hours of intensive questioning and a thorough search of our car. Unfortunately, Mr. Nkabinde had several documents in his possession relating to his denomination's work in Mozambique. This raised suspicion because the ANC had a base in that country, which was used as a springboard for military excursions into South Africa. They suspected any black with extensive contacts in Mozambique of being an ANC ally. I was also suspect because my diary listed speaking engagements at Wits University, where I addressed the subject of the detention laws. I had been asked to speak on this subject because of my work at Youth Alive and because I encountered many young people who experienced the full humiliation of these laws.

The police at the road block thought this was a great coup. They were elated at their "catch" and pleased to have finally uncovered the link that would prove the connection with George and the ANC. In truth, I knew nothing of George's specific activities with the ANC. George had been very careful not to put me, my family and my ministry with Youth Alive in any compromising positions.

The one time George did come to my home was on the evening of the day my mother went into a coma. He was agitated because he knew about our mother's illness and wanted to see her before she died. He was also under pressure to flee South Africa that night because the passport he was using expired at midnight.

The same evening that George visited with our mother, I helped him to return to Swaziland. We drove down every back road that I knew between Johannesburg and the Swaziland border. It was a nine-hour, danger-fraught journey to and from the border, and we were never sure when a patrol might suddenly stop us. When we said our farewells I was not sure when and where I would ever see my brother again. I finally returned home to Chumi in the small hours, the roads now empty of traffic. I collapsed into bed, exhausted but pleased that I had seen George go safely across the border. Our mother died soon after.

The police at the road block were able to learn nothing from us. And although they eventually let me and my friends proceed, that incident was not the last time that George's activities in the ANC would directly impact my family.

On December 16, 1979, George was arrested by South Africa's Security Special Branch (SSB). During one of the cross-border raids by the South African defense forces into Mozambique, the regional base of the ANC was attacked and documents listing all of the ANC operatives within South Africa were confiscated. George's name and activities were immediately uncovered. All that remained was for them to find someone who could identify George. This they were able to do. One of the SSBs had managed to infiltrate the ANC. He knew our family and could easily identify George.

My brother was arrested near the home of one of our relatives. His arrest marked the beginning of many months of interrogation, torture and loneliness. To keep his whereabouts secret and to confuse him psychologically, the police shuttled him from prison to prison. Neither he nor his family or friends knew where he would be at any given moment.

Chumi and I learned of George's arrest when we were awakened by a loud bang on the front door of our home at two o'clock in the morning. My wife and I jumped out of bed and peered through the window, only to be blinded by flashlights shining directly into our eyes. We knew there was trouble when we saw four vehicles parked outside and the house surrounded by security forces with rifles. It took me several minutes to put on my artificial leg. The banging on the door got louder. No sooner had I opened the door than every room in the house was occupied by two policemen. I was called back to the bedroom where Chumi sat frightened on the bed. There, the officers told me to get dressed; they were taking me away. I tried to find out where they were taking me, but I was told it was none of my business. The last thing I said to my wife before leaving was that she should inform Cyril Ramaphosa. As I was being escorted from the bedroom, I saw they had thoroughly searched the house; papers and books lay strewn all over the floor.

I was hustled out into the night and driven to Protea, a regional security headquarters on the west side of Soweto. I had no idea if I would ever see Chumi and our first-born son, Lebogang, again. On top of this, Chumi was now expecting our second child and was well on in her pregnancy. I feared the shock of the night's events might provoke a miscarriage. Mercifully, this did not happen.

From Protea police headquarters I was taken to the Sunnyside Police Station cells in Pretoria, an hour's journey away. The officers' purpose in detaining me was to get me to furnish them with the evidence to incriminate George. I was being implicated with my brother in acts of sabotage that, if proven, would have made me a co-conspirator and earned me a lengthy jail sentence.

When the police failed to get a confession out of me, they tried to get me to turn state's witness against my brother in a written statement linking George to a recent bombing of the Orlando East police station. They threatened me with contempt of court if I refused to cooperate. If I had turned state's witness against my brother, it would have been the worst form of betrayal. I would never have been able to face George, and I never would have been trusted by anyone in the black community again.

After two weeks of continued interrogation and harassment, the police let me go. What saved me from possible physical torture was the arrival of Dr. David Bosch, professor of missiology at the University of South Africa (UNISA). Dr. Bosch demanded that I have access to a lawyer and a medical doctor. At the same time a telegram campaign was started by alumni who knew me from Wheaton Graduate School in Wheaton, Illinois. The telegrams to the minister of police demanded that I either be charged or released. I believe this international pressure forced my interrogators not to use violence.

Over the next few weeks the police detained all of my brothers, one at a time, for several hours of questioning. Police efforts to implicate George failed. They finally let all my brothers go. However, my own two-week incarceration will live with me forever.

My welcome to prison life began with a tall Afrikaner sergeant who said to me in broken English: "Welcome to the chamber of horrors." From this macabre beginning things only got worse. I could sense this man had had many detainees in his "care" and that gentleness was not his trademark.

I was searched and my personal belongings removed and put in storage. I was thrown immediately into solitary confinement without even my Bible. My nights were spent lying on three dirty blankets, sharing them with large bed bugs that attacked me as soon as the lights were out. The blankets served both as a bed and a covering on the rough concrete floor. Thankfully, it was summer, and very hot, and I could throw off the filthy blankets. During the days, when I was not being interrogated, I would stand under the cold-water shower and sing hymns and freedom songs.

In the cell next to mine lived a man who had spent six months in solitary confinement without any human contact except for his interrogators. When I sang freedom songs he joined in. In this way I knew there was someone to whom I could be an encouragement even in that horrible situation.

Talking was forbidden and this rule was strictly enforced, so we could talk only late at night between rounds of the guards. We had already been told that if we were caught speaking we would be placed in different cells. Each time we talked we knew we were taking a great risk, and we knew that it might be the last conversation we would ever have. Even so, we spent many hours standing on our toilet seats talking through a small narrow window with a metal grill set high in the thick concrete wall. We never once caught sight of each other. The prison builders had done their job well.

In hushed tones, with one ear listening for the heavy-booted footsteps of the guards, we would talk late into the night, on every conceivable subject. I shared my faith with him and he shared with me the difficulties he had understanding Jesus. He, like so many blacks, had rejected the defaced Christ of the whites, who was identified with the oppressor and was not able to identify with his pain. In this prison there was no room for a faith that ignored issues of justice and righteousness. I resolved all the more, whether I was in or out of prison, to seek to be faithful to the Christ of Scripture rather than to a culturally conformed Christ who served the interests of the rich and ignored the plight of the poor and oppressed.

The reality of God's all-encompassing love and power was forcefully brought home to me after I started to slide into a depression four days after being incarcerated. The experience that followed helped to sustain me during the rest of my detention.

After four days in solitary confinement, I was facing my first Sunday in prison. Sunday was the day that I normally would have spent with my Christian friends, leading the congregation of Ebenezer Evangelical Church. During Sunday afternoons in Soweto I would go from one Youth Alive meeting to the next, doing what I enjoyed so much—talking with young people about Christ. This is when the prison walls became unbearable. They were more than a physical barrier; they totally excluded me from Christian fellowship of any kind. I became very depressed. For the first time, I felt extremely lonely. It was hard to sing a hymn or pray. My lips felt like clay. I could not sing the songs of praise to God.

As I lay on the cell floor, I suddenly heard the distant sound of church bells, and I climbed onto the toilet seat to look through the narrow window. I strained to look through the wire mesh, at last glimpsing a distant church steeple. The sight reassured me that there was more to life than the seemingly unconquerable evil that had imprisoned me.

A mental picture of thousands of Christians meeting together in churches all over South Africa began to form in my mind. I thought of the many churches I had preached in. I thought of SACLA—the South Africa Christian Leadership Assembly—held in July 1979 not very far from this prison. I thought of all the young people in Youth Alive. I thought of my wife, Chumi, and our son getting ready for church, and I realized that my name would be mentioned in prayer that very morning. I bowed my head and thanked God that I was part of his church regardless of my physical circumstances.

I have no idea how long I looked at that steeple. After what seemed like an hour, I lowered myself to the floor, having assured myself that the church would ultimately triumph over the gates of this and any other hell.

At three o'clock one morning, I was awakened and taken out of my prison cell by the guards. This was the usual practice on interrogation days. But instead of being taken to the interrogation cell, I was marched into the police captain's office and told to wait. I was kept in the office for four hours, completely alone, with guards posted outside the door. The captain finally arrived at 8:30 and asked me if I had any complaints against the police. I knew then that I was being released or I was going to be transferred to another prison. I asked him which of these two alternatives was the case. He told me I was going home.

I knew that a complaint would have delayed my release. It would take up to half a day for a magistrate to come to the prison and take my statement. Because I just wanted to get out of there, I made no complaints, and I was released. The truly regrettable thing was that I was not able to say goodbye to my faceless friend in the next cell.

My detention appeared as a front-page story in the *Sunday Times,* Johannesburg's leading Sunday newspaper at that time. After my release I realized how fortunate I was, considering how others such as Frank Chikane, general secretary of the South African Council of Churches, and

Cyril Ramaphosa had been tortured and confined far longer than I had been. I counted my blessings.

I learned much later that Chumi had been deeply affected by my imprisonment. She had been told nothing as to where, why or how long I was being detained. My incarceration gave both of us a brief look at what wives of prisoners suffered when, because of the detention laws, husbands were whisked away by security police, never to be heard from again. Now my release brought great joy to my family and to my co-workers at Youth Alive.

The sun was rising over Soweto as the police dropped me off at my home. Chumi was surprised and overjoyed. I was free. It was the start of a new day.

14

A Brother on Trial

Nine ANC members went on trial August 4, 1980, at the Palace of Justice in Pretoria. My brother George was Accused Number Four. Justice Jaap de Villiers was the presiding judge. Because of the gravity of the charges and the possible length of the trial, the judge worked with two assessors. In South Africa there is no jury system.

The first day of the trial opened with a packed courtroom and very tight security. The national and international media were on hand. Our whole family was present as well. Armed guards were everywhere, creating an atmosphere of hostility.

A hush came over the court as the accused filed in. All nine were being charged with high treason by reason of being ANC members and willfully seeking the overthrow of the state by violence. The penalty, if they were found guilty, was death.

The charges against George included: "Receiving military training in Angola; performing acts of warfare, undermining and sabotage against the Republic of South Africa; and reconnoitering and planning an attack on gas storage tanks in Waltloo near Pretoria with a view to blowing them up." He was also accused of "being in possession of and stocking supplies of weapons, ammunition and explosives for purposes of warfare against the state."

The charges also linked George with the other indicted ANC members and included the fire bombing of two police stations in Soweto and one north of Pretoria; George had supplied the explosives making the bombings possible.

111

Linked with the police- station bombings was a bank shoot-out in which three of George's ANC comrades died and a number of whites were killed.

In charging all nine men with high treason, murder and membership in a banned organization, the state invoked the law of "Common Cause." This law allows police to prosecute individuals even if those individuals did not participate in the actual execution of the crime. All the state has to do is prove that the individuals concerned were involved in the planning and agreed to its execution.

The most serious single charge against George was his intention to blow up the gas storage tanks.

When they caught George, police found notes he had made while reconnoitering the area. It was clear from these notes that he was planning to blow up the tanks in such a way that no human lives would be taken. Death was not part of his agenda for anyone. As the charge was read I remembered how George used to say that he was not a butcher, that he could never see himself killing people. But the line between violence and legitimate force is so fine that it was hard for me to know if and when he had ever crossed it.

Mr. Jules Browde, the counsel engaged to defend the nine, argued that the actions of the nine did not constitute "extreme cases." He referred to evidence by the eminent sociologist F. A. Maritz, who found the nine men to be "comparatively gentle people." This was certainly true of my brother. Professor Maritz also found no inherent evil in the accused and he stressed that they became enmeshed in the activities of the ANC largely because of their youthful, rebellious nature. He observed that in many cases the rebel of today became the leader of tomorrow. The question was: What had to be done when a rebel disobeyed the law and was caught?

There was no doubt in the judge's mind with respect to that question. On November 26, three and a half months later, the accused entered the courtroom for their final sentencing. They were singing freedom songs, something

112

they had done every day of the trial. My brother led the singing as they climbed the fifteen steps to the dock to hear the judge pass sentence.

The judge announced his verdict in Afrikaans and the court interpreter, who was black, translated it into Zulu for the prisoners: Accused One, Two and Three were convicted of high treason and given the death sentence.

I had never heard a death sentence passed on anyone before, and my stomach knotted when I heard the judge say: "Do you have anything to say before I pronounce the death sentence on you?" One of the accused thanked both the judge and a policeman who had treated him "like a human being."

The first three sat down without any sign of emotion. It seemed as if the severity of the sentence had not registered. They looked numb. The judge granted all three leave to appeal the convictions and sentence.

When it came time for my brother's sentence, George stood up and faced the judge. I watched him closely. It seemed as if his knees would not hold him and he would collapse. Somehow he held up and stood there in silence, waiting for his sentence.

A hush descended over the court. The judge cleared his throat and said: "Because you've shown that you are a very intelligent person and understood clearly what you were doing, and because you did not carry out your intentions, I sentence you to twenty years in prison." I looked over at my father and the other family members. They all looked dazed. It didn't seem to register in anyone's mind that George had not been given the death sentence. He would live. We hardly heard the rest of the sentences—jail terms ranging from ten to twenty years each.

At the end, all the convicted men turned and faced the courtroom and raised their fists in defiance. They then turned to face the gallery, where black people stood up and sang the hauntingly beautiful Xhosa hymn "Nkosi Sikelel' i-Afrika"—"God Bless Africa"—which had become the ANC anthem and the anthem of at least three independent countries in East and Central Africa.

It was a long ride back home to Soweto. In our minds we were beginning to gear ourselves up for the few visits that we would be allowed to make with George in prison. We knew that all the convicted men would go to the infamous Robben Island except numbers One, Two and Three, who would go to death row. (Their sentences were later commuted to life imprisonment in exchange for the names of the mercenaries involved in an unsuccessful coup attempt in the Seychelles.)

Robben Island is an island prison fourteen miles west of Cape Town, surrounded by shark-infested waters of the south Atlantic Ocean. This prison was home to Nelson Mandela and other well-known, convicted ANC political prisoners.

As my family returned home, my mind reflected on the events of the last few months. George had chosen the violent option. In the deepest recesses of my heart I knew I could not go that way. My way would not be that of the zealot.

But neither would I bow the knee before the oppressive ways of the white government or turn a blind eye to immoral apartheid laws. I would work for change—change by the grace of God—within the system of oppression that dominated my people. It would be the nonviolent way of Jesus.

The cry of Moses for the enslaved Israelites would be my cry: Let my people go. And only God in his providence could answer that cry. In the meantime, I would pray patiently and grow in my own faith in fear and trembling. I saw no other way but the way of love and the cross.

15

The Church Speaks Out

*For our struggle is not against flesh and
blood, but against the powers of this dark
world and against the spiritual forces of
evil in the heavenly realms. Therefore
put on the full armor of God, so that when
the day of evil comes, you may be able to
stand your ground, and after you have
done everything, to stand.*

Ephesians (Chapter 6, verses 12-13)

It would not be long before my prayers for increased church
involvement in the black struggle would begin to be answered—though not without setbacks and frustration.

One of the first major Christian conferences that sought to
wrestle with the hard issues was the South African Christian
Leadership Assembly (SACLA), held in 1979. But difficulties were present from the outset.

When SACLA was first proposed, there was enormous
opposition to evangelical participation from organizations
such as the South African Fellowship of Evangelicals.
SACLA was viewed by conservative Evangelicals as politically liberal and unbiblical. My presence, as the only black
Evangelical serving on the executive committee of SACLA,
was seen by many as a betrayal of the evangelical community.

At the end of the first day of conference planning, the white
Evangelicals in attendance came together and declared that

SACLA was not a truly evangelical effort; they did not feel comfortable staying. They said they would come to the conference if invited, but they would not remain members of the executive committee. In their minds, the issue was quite simple: you were either an Evangelical (equated in their minds with Christians who supported the South African status quo) or you were an ecumenical (a theologically questionable Christian, with probable ties to Communism, who was striving for a nonracial South Africa). The two never mixed, and the reason was as clear as black and white.

Western missionaries, in most cases, came out of a very conservative-fundamentalist theological background, which believed that anything not sanctioned by their denomination and taught in their Bible schools was unbiblical. On that basis SACLA was condemned by missionary groups. Anything outside the realm of evangelism—especially anything that smacked of politics—was outside the orb of discussion.

Like the missionary, the black pastor had been taught that he had only one concern—evangelism, the saving of souls. It was not his place to get involved in politics. Such activity would only distract him from his main calling and would be "unspiritual." The physical body and whatever happened to it was largely irrelevant; the soul was everything. The state, after all, was ordained of God, and Christians were called to be obedient to its demands.

My hopes were not entirely shattered however. A small group of deeply committed young black leaders emerged from within SACLA. I was hopeful that together, through SACLA, we could mobilize the church to a point where we could really make a statement about racism to all of South Africa. At the same time we hoped SACLA would empower the church to minister and evangelize, to involve itself in community projects and student work, and to be a meaningful voice of conscience to the South African government.

These were the hopes we nursed; and when leaders such as Anglican Bishop Desmond Tutu spoke at SACLA, we found we shared the same dream. For the first time in the history of

South Africa, right here in Pretoria, the political and religious heart of South Africa, a minor revolution was taking place. Blacks were given unrestricted access to white residential areas and hotels for the duration of the conference. They were openly invited to white homes. These were actions hitherto unheard of. SACLA had broken new ground.

SACLA clarified the issues without further alienating the already estranged communities. The truth was spoken by both blacks and whites in love, and sometimes in fear. The fears of whites and the anger and mistrust of blacks were openly discussed. One of the greatest achievements of SACLA was the dialogue between black and white university students. Out of this developed the Student Union for Christian Action which exists to this day.

Sadly, SACLA was to be a small flame in the darkness, soon snuffed out. SACLA had been too unsettling an experience for many.

The religious right, a fragmented and reactionary group in South Africa, was suddenly galvanized by their fear of SACLA. They now came together and sought to disrupt and, if possible, destroy SACLA. They perceived SACLA as a threat to their faith and conservative politics. They saw black aspirations as "communist" and incompatible with the Christian gospel.

Theirs was a mandate that married the gospel of Christ to apartheid politics and free-wheeling capitalism. Anything that eroded the privileges they enjoyed under European colonial rule was portrayed as coming from Satan. Emerging black leaders in independent Africa were seen not as nationalist leaders dispensing with colonial rule, but as agents of evil.

With the disappointing conclusion of the SACLA conference, I was reminded of an earlier conference where the same distancing occurred. This conference was called PACLA, the Pan African Conference Leadership Assembly. It was held in Nairobi in 1976. PACLA was a follow-up

117

of the Lausanne Congress on Evangelism held in Switzerland in 1974, the first major gathering of thoughtful evangelical Christians drawn from almost every country in the world. On my return to South Africa in 1976 I had been invited almost immediately to attend PACLA.

As my friends and I made our way to the conference, a situation arose which highlighted the very problems we were facing.

We arrived at Nairobi Airport to find that white South Africans were being refused permission to enter the country, whereas blacks were being allowed in without visas. The political tables had suddenly been turned.

Immediately we felt that this was not right and appealed the decision to the authorities. Our appeal was so effective that the decision was overruled and black and white South Africans all went into the conference together. However, there was political fallout from this incident, and tension arose at the conference as a result. The unsettling aspect of all this was the uncanny way it mirrored South Africa.

It was a revelation to me to experience this reversal of roles on the continent of Africa. Suddenly whites were in a position of weakness and we blacks were in a position of privilege and strength. The question for me was: Do I take advantage of this sudden acquired privileged status and lord it over the whites? Or, do I as a black Christian overcome evil with good and love the oppressors? As a Christian, I had only one true option: reach out in love on behalf of Jesus Christ. Any real privilege any of us had came from being children of God and had nothing to do with the color of our skin.

The situation underscored for me the problems we faced in trying to get South African white Christians to give up their privileged status. They are totally threatened by the thought. They are not able to go anywhere else in the world and have the same privileges they have in South Africa. Therefore, they do everything in their power to slow the rate of progress.

Once we arrived at the PACLA conference, a second tension arose. The black evangelical missionary church, founded by the white missionary enterprise, and the ecumenical community that was sympathetic to the black cause were at odds. As a Bible-believing black Evangelical I had much in common with the first group, though I had serious misgivings about white missionary control of black Christians. Like the black Evangelicals, I had serious questions about much ecumenical theology that was blatantly unbiblical; yet these same ecumenicals stood for justice and righteousness in a way that Evangelicals did not.

The breakthrough came when Professor David Bosch openly spoke about the dilemma of the Afrikaner church in South Africa. He publicly confessed his and his fellow churchmembers' guilt in their lack of opposition to apartheid and asked for forgiveness. His confession stunned everyone. Later, those of us from the black community in South Africa accepted the need for reconciliation, and we met during the conference to work out the implications of David Bosch's challenging message. We all agreed to continue the dialogue when we returned home.

The point at which I personally experienced the greatest polarization between ecumenical and Evangelical was at SACEL, the South African Conference for Evangelical Leaders, which was held near Pretoria, in 1985.

As a plenary speaker, I was called on to "defend the gospel" by speaking against liberation theology, African theology and black theology. I refused. I said the gospel is its own defense and required none from me. I said I had not come to the conference to cut down other theological positions in order to boost my own.

I cited an old Afrikaner proverb that said, "You don't do your dirty laundry in someone else's dirty laundry water." Even if these theologies had inherent weaknesses, we would not make our theology any stronger by exposing and railing against their weaknesses. Therefore, I would not boost evangelical theology by looking at others and saying, "Look how weak you are."

I told the group, "Let us try to find out whether or not we can learn from these other theologies. Why are these theologies so popular?" Obviously these theologies dealt with what people had perceived were critical questions regarding justice and how the poor should be treated. In light of this, what should evangelical theologians be doing and saying? Were we asking the right questions for our communities? Were we really showing Jesus as the answer to questions of injustice, racial hatred, fear and oppression? We could only do this, I said, if we were prepared to ask the hard questions.

After I argued my case, the director of Frontline Fellowship, an extreme right-wing organization, stood up and said, "Nobody in his right mind should take Caesar seriously." I was speechless. He then said, "I know Dr. Tokumbo Adeyemo, general secretary of the Association of Evangelicals of Africa and Madagascar. And I would like this conference to know that what Caesar is saying is not a view held by other African evangelical leaders. Dr. Adeyemo, whom you all know, would never agree with the way Caesar analyzes these different theologies."

The director then went on to quote various evangelical statements, many of them taken completely out of context, that were anti-liberation theology, anti-black theology and anti-African theology. He said, "You see, this is what Evangelicals are saying. Now, let us all agree that Caesar is no longer one of us. That is why he is not prepared to hit out against his buddies."

I was totally devastated. I felt betrayed by people that I thought would at least have listened to me and tried to understand, even if they disagreed. All I had wanted to do was avoid condemning another's point of view. I had not said I agreed with all the other theologies; I simply could not denounce them with generalized, sweeping statements. There was much truth in those theologies, but to have tried to sort it all out in that context would have left me wide open to charges of heresy.

120

I would not defend myself. Others rose up and supported what I had said.

One supporter was Jim Johnston, the pastor of Bedford-view Chapel and former director of the Student Christian Association. He pointed out that the reason there was such a negative response to what I was saying was that people in the conference were not in touch with their own fears. This was true. Most Evangelicals were living in denial of the reality of South Africa. They were still afraid of the possibility of black rule.

At the conclusion of this session of the conference, David Howard, executive director of the World Evangelical Fellowship, spoke with me at length. He tried to encourage me and bolster my sagging spirits. He noted that the entire negative response to what I said came from expatriate missionaries.

I never felt more isolated from people whom I thought were my brothers in Christ. After that session David Howard, Aubrey Adams (a close personal friend) and I left the conference together in sadness.

16
New Tests of Faith

I left the SACEL conference feeling very depressed and let down. I had been betrayed. My faith had been called into question, my loyalties challenged. I felt I had lost the initiative with my black brothers. Worse, I had been attacked by a white man and he had invoked the spirit of a leading black Christian—my brother in the faith—against me.

Somehow I had failed to convey to the conference my compassion for other points of view while holding on to my own commitment to Jesus Christ and social justice. I passionately believed in the gospel of God's redeeming grace, but I was not prepared to accept an otherworldly spirituality that ignored social inequalities and allowed rampant racism practiced by people who called themselves Christians. Nor was I going to accept those whites who wrapped themselves in the flag and waved Bibles in the name of the Father, Son and Holy Ghost—while shooting blacks as alleged Communists.

Never! Never would I accept the injustices of white South African society or a theology that said three quarters of South Africa's population were less in God's eyes because of the color of their skin. Jesus is Lord of all—black, white, the economic system, the political system, the church—or he is Lord of nothing.

I was glad not to be driving home alone to Soweto. With me were David Howard and Aubrey Adams. We were exhausted emotionally and spiritually as we drove down the highway toward Soweto. We just wanted to get home and forget about what had happened at the conference.

We started to talk after we entered Soweto. As we drove along the dusty unpaved streets I was reminded again of the physical contrast with Pretoria with its tree-lined, paved streets. My own humiliation at the conference now seemed to match the humiliating world of the black township in which I was forced to live. Resentment built up inside me and I had to ask God to help me forgive both what I had experienced and the place I was forced to come back to.

I took the long road home so I could show David, for whom this was a first visit to Soweto, some of the realities of the township. I wanted him to understand what I had tried to say at the conference.

We were driving along one of the back roads leading to my home when suddenly we came across the sight of Phafogang High School burning fiercely from end to end. Flames were leaping up into the late afternoon sky as smoke poured from smashed windows. There were no students in sight, which seemed odd for that time of day. Normally there would have been about 2,000 students present. But the area was empty.

Later we learned that when the fire had broken out the army quickly rolled into the area and everyone had scattered to the four winds. No one in their right minds wanted to face the prospect of being shot by a highly armed militia.

Under the circumstances, I should have been more careful. I knew I should not have been driving with foreigners through an army-controlled area. By now it was too late. I was already in the middle of a security zone. I dropped my speed but kept driving. We were all feeling a bit afraid. Even David, who had never been in a black township before, felt the fear and tension in the air.

A security car of the military intelligence spotted us and began to follow us, but we made it home without incident. I didn't want to tell David what might have happened had we been stopped.

My joy was short-lived. Hardly had we settled down with a

cup of tea when two armored vehicles full of soldiers pulled up in front of our home. Within seconds soldiers had sprung off their vehicles and surrounded the house. Four of them immediately entered our home by the front door that I had unaccountably left open.

They came up to me and asked for my identification. After learning who I was, one of them proceeded to radio headquarters and announce in Afrikaans: "I have tracked the man down." While we waited for the soldier to finish his radio call to headquarters, the other soldiers briefly interrogated us. Three of the soldiers stood at the ready with their rifles. It was a clear warning for us not to move.

They demanded to know who the "white man" was. David explained who he was and what he was doing there. They demanded to see his passport. David produced it with the separate visa for South African entry, but the soldier wasn't willing to recognize it or the passport. Another round of hurried talks took place between the officer and headquarters. Finally he was convinced that David's passport was legitimate.

The officer then spotted David's camera and wanted to know if David had taken photographs of any military police or security situations during all the stops they said they had seen us make. David said no. Fortunately David's film had not had even one frame exposed. The police were forced by the evidence to believe his story.

Yet despite everything we said they were not convinced that what we told them was the whole truth. They insisted that we would have to come with them to headquarters. They radioed ahead to say they were bringing us in, and they were instructed to bring everyone except Chumi.

The soldiers did make one concession: after assigning two soldiers to ride with us, they allowed us to drive our own car between their two vehicles. It was a strange thing to do by military standards but we did not protest. They clearly could see we posed no armed threat.

At the station we were taken upstairs and interrogated by a

125

plainclothes Afrikaner officer. He was sarcastic and bitter in his questioning of David and asked him why he had a separate U.S. passport. David explained that in order to get into other African countries he could not have a South African visa in his passport.

"Yes," sneered the officer. "They think we all have leprosy."

The officer freely spoke his mind. He knew the prevailing attitude of African states. Those states would not permit a person to come into their country if their passports indicated they had been in or done business with South Africa.

Then the officer turned to me and asked, "Who are you?"

"I am Caesar Molebatsi," I said.

"Do you have your I.D. with you to prove that?"

We had been hustled quickly out of the house and I had not had time to pick it up. "No," I said.

"In that case, we'll just have to detain the whole lot of you. It's 4:00 p.m. and it's time for me to leave," he said.

It was Friday. If they locked us up, we would not be attended to until Monday morning. We would have to spend the entire weekend in the police station. I began to protest strongly, knowing what an uncomfortable weekend awaited me and my friends if we were detained in a flea-infested cell.

"Forget it," I said. "I'm not going to be locked up for a whole weekend in the cells. If you are going to detain us, it must be on the authority of Brigadier Coetzee."

Brigadier Coetzee was the police commander whom I had met during negotiations before one of the big political funerals in Soweto. Coetzee told the group I was with that if ever we had a problem with the police we should phone him. On this particular day I decided to take full advantage of that offer. I stood my ground.

I knew we could be detained under section 29, a law which allows the police to hold people while possible charges are investigated. They could have locked me up and thrown away the key, but the mention of the brigadier's name put a damper on their decision to lock us up.

While I was having this conversation with the policeman, his staff summoned the security officer in charge of the sector where I lived. He came into the room and seemed very pleased at my capture.

"We've been looking for you," he said. "We have a wheelbarrow full of files on you. Now you will have to give us some answers."

Before he could go any further I blurted out, "Okay, now I'm here. What are your questions? You can't hold us here without good cause. We have broken no laws."

While this new discussion was going on, the other officer continued paging the man who was to interrogate me officially. They had people assigned for different duties; the interrogator who was assigned to religious leaders was not available.

In a threatening voice the security officer said, "We are not going to let you go. You are going to have to wait here until the interrogator comes."

"When is he coming?" I asked.

"Monday," they said.

"Forget it. I'm going home."

I began to get up. A policeman shoved me back into my seat. I knew then I had pushed them as far as I could.

In the meantime, they had taken David and Aubrey out to another room for further interrogation. After cross-examining them the police let them go. They returned David's passport and camera.

They kept me, however, and continued to grill me with more questions. As the police had no idea what the official interrogator was going to ask me they plied me with all kinds of stupid questions. They wanted to know about different people I knew. What was my attitude toward what Bishop Tutu was saying publicly about apartheid, and did I agree with him? "What do you think about the ANC? What is your position on violence?" On and on they went.

Finally I realized they had no way of legitimately detaining me, so I challenged them once again to clear their actions with

Brigadier Coetzee.

The captain at last felt so intimidated by the thought of a brigadier coming to the police station that he ordered my release. He told me that I should not leave the area as they might want to call me in at short notice to interrogate me further. I was not about to argue with him.

I left the police station and found David and Aubrey waiting anxiously outside for me. As I looked at my watch I realized they had been waiting for me for more than three hours. They were tremendously relieved to see me; they had almost given up hope of returning home with me.

This arrest galvanized David, who had been embarrassed at the accusations made against me at the SACEL conference. He now realized what life was like for a black person in Soweto, and he understood that I could not divorce politics from my life or faith.

Jesus came to proclaim freedom for the prisoners and recovery of sight for the blind, and to set at liberty those who are oppressed. It was my duty and obligation to preach this message and to deal with all aspects of life—social, spiritual and political—and not to divorce them from each other.

I would live or die, be jailed or be free, believing in the ultimate triumph of God over personal and corporate evil. In the meantime I would remain where God had put me and live out his truth for those around me.

17
Room for New Voices

On the evening of June 12, 1986, a number of concerned people met at my home in Soweto to discuss the potential disruption of the upcoming Soweto Day celebrations on June 16, the tenth anniversary of the killing of Hector Petersen.

Massive rallies were being planned to commemorate the riots of 1976. There were great expectations. Tension filled the air because huge numbers were anticipated at these rallies. The first six months of this year had been the bloodiest since June 1976, and the fear of police intimidation lurked in everyone's mind. There were rumors that the government would clamp down with the harshest emergency regulations ever.

The government found itself in a dilemma. To allow the rallies to go ahead would only show the extent of the power and organization of the black political movement. On the other hand to have a massive military and police presence at these rallies would invite a blood bath. The government resolved this dilemma by announcing on June 14 the harshest state-of-emergency regulations since 1976. This announcement stunned the black community with its severity.

In protest, a movement arose that threatened to hit the government at one of its most vulnerable points. One of the local political organizations suggested that citizens refuse to pay rent to the local black authorities responsible for the thousands of government houses in the black townships.

Many black people hated these local authorities because they ruthlessly collected exorbitant sums of money from poor people in the guise of administering the townships. These authorities were viewed in much the same way that the poor in Jesus' time viewed Jewish tax collectors who ruthlessly collected large sums of money for their Roman bosses. These local authorities merely did the bidding of white officials, carrying out the policies of the apartheid government.

Overnight, graffiti appeared on walls all over Soweto urging residents not to pay their rent as a sign of protest. The idea immediately caught on. Many people discussed it in trains, buses and shopping centers, and thousands more began to wonder aloud why they had never thought about doing this before. It was the easiest way to cripple the money supply of the state machinery and strip local black counselors of their power. The rent boycotts would mean no money to pay exorbitant salaries and insurance policies, including the "inconvenience" bonuses—paid to white officials who "endangered" their lives by coming into the black community every day and to black councillors who collaborated with the government.

The rent boycotts spread, and they continued long past the June 16 Soweto Day anniversary. In spite of cuts in the electricity supply, garbage piling up on street corners and sewage spilling out onto the streets for lack of maintenance, the resolve of the black community prevailed. Within four years the city council was more than half-a-billion rand in debt. Townships like Soweto found themselves in debt to the electricity supplier responsible for all South Africa. Smaller townships suffered even more.

The boycotts were clearly affecting the establishment. It became clear to the government that negotiations were necessary. But the process was fraught with tension and setbacks. And wherever negotiations broke down, violence inevitably erupted.

The government learned two bitter lessons. The first was that it could not force people to do anything against their will without causing death and destruction. Second, black people could effectively wield economic power as a form of protest.

130

The hope that the government would rely solely on negotiation rather than force failed, however. Even though negotiations are even now taking place, that period between 1986 and 1990 was marred by horrible acts of violence.

I witnessed one incident I shall never forget.

On the evening of August 10, 1987, in a township called White City, just two blocks from my home, the army swooped into the area and cordoned off the streets. Soldiers moved from house to house demanding that the residents either produce the receipts proving payment of rent or undertake to make payments by signing an agreement with the local authorities. The residents resisted, refusing to pay the rent or sign the agreement. I watched as thirty of them were dragged from their homes and shot to death. It was plain murder by the organized forces of the apartheid government. But no one was charged with murder; the killings had state sanction.

The local authorities were never allowed to forget that massacre. It served to radicalize the local communities, and people resolved never to pay rent until all the grievances were met.

After the brutal crackdown in 1976 a crescendo of voices had been heard from across the political and religious spectrum crying out against the suppression of black political expression. After the massacre of August 10, 1987, a number of important new voices were heard on the South African political landscape and three important documents were published.

A multiracial group of clergy calling themselves Ministers United for Christian Co-Responsibility (MUCCOR) issued a "Challenge to the Church," a theological comment on the political crisis in South Africa. It became known as the "Kairos Document." The document stated in blunt terms that the "apartheid regime is clearly tyrannical. It is therefore a morally illegitimate regime and should be replaced by a government that will govern in the interests of all the people."

The document condemned what it called "State Theology": "Everyone who disobeys and opposes the State is called a godless, atheistic Communist. And the State's idea of hell on earth would be a future communist take-over." The document boldly declared that "the god that the State preaches to us is not the God of the Bible. It is an idol." The Kairos Document went on to say that hope was possible for both the oppressor and oppressed because the gospel was a message of hope: "There is hope because God has promised us in Jesus Christ that justice and truth and love will triumph over all injustice and oppression in the end."

Although some churches within South Africa responded very negatively, and white evangelical churches denounced the document as communist propaganda, more than 200 international clergy and leaders signed the document. Christians both Protestant and Roman Catholic, ecumenical and evangelical—from South Africa, Namibia, South Korea, the Philippines, El Salvador, Nicaragua and Guatemala—affirmed the document. It became the rallying point for thousands of people within these churches. It could not be ignored.

A second voice which could be heard was the National Initiative for Reconciliation (NIR). This organization brought together more than 400 pastors, theologians and leaders of parachurch groups. I was invited to be among those who first met in Pietermaritzburg in September 1986 to try to answer a critical question: What do we as a church believe God is telling us to do in the face of South African violence and government intransigence? This meeting was important because of the large delegation from the Dutch Reformed church, which up to this time had supported the South African government. We hoped that meaningful dialogue would begin.

We were successful. Days of dialogue resulted in numerous declarations by the synods of the Dutch Reformed church condemning apartheid. In November 1990, at the National Conference of Churches in Rustenberg, the Dutch

Reformed church went even further and accepted the principle of restitution.

Since its first meeting, the NIR has had significant impact on the white community. It initiated an ongoing program of education for white people who ordinarily would not have been exposed to the painful reality of apartheid policies. This was welcomed by many of us who had been struggling in our ministry of reconciliation. If ordinary white South Africans could see how ordinary black South Africans were being discriminated against just because of their skin color, it might help them to face the evil of apartheid on a more personal level.

The NIR provided the building blocks that we could use to help white people be obedient to God and fight the evil of the system. From that 1986 conference came a number of broad initiatives, actions and responses that had the potential to bring about reconciliation between black and white. They included mounting an interchurch evangelistic campaign with a strong interracial component; starting a prayer group for revival, healing and justice in South Africa; and planning public events of united Christian witness or prayer in local town or city halls.

At the church level, initiatives were suggested that included organizing interracial dialogue and/or Bible study groups, planning pulpit exchanges between black and white ministers, and having white church members spend a night with a black Christian family in the township in order to see the conditions around them.

Other initiatives included projects in education—raising funds for improving black education; initiating involvement in Aid and Development projects to assist the poor; mounting job-creation schemes with churches on an interracial basis.

The cry for freedom could now be understood and undergirded by the church and would not be silenced by government troops in the townships or by President Botha's bitter denunciations. Being a member of a trade union, involving oneself in political marches and praying prayers that specifically demanded the demise of the South African government were now being legitimized within the ecumenical churches.

As an Evangelical who was deeply involved with MUCCOR and the formation of the Kairos Document, I became increasingly burdened by the lack of greater evangelical involvement in justice issues. I found myself walking a lonely road sandwiched between ecumenicals on the one hand and pietistic-separatists on the other.

It was a real answer to my own prayers when a few other black Evangelicals began meeting with me on a weekly basis to pray for and be accountable to one another. We did not want to slip away from the moorings of an evangelical faith based on the authority of Scripture; at the same time we could not ignore the blatant injustices all around us that demanded a biblical response. Our group became known as Concerned Evangelicals (CE).

We were primarily black Christians who were products of white mission agencies. All mission agencies were run by white missionaries who represented every conceivable theological tradition and denominational stripe in the world, coming from different nations and diverse cultural backgrounds. But they had one thing in common: they were incapable of transmitting to their mission churches a theology which began with blacks and their needs, spoken from within their context, in a form relevant to their culture. Everything had been imposed from the outside without asking what the black Christian wanted or needed. Concerned Evangelicals believed that something had to be done to help these evangelical Christians deal with the crises appearing on the horizon.

The first crisis was our identity. Who were we? What did we believe? As a group of black Christians who had acknowledged and accepted Jesus Christ as our Lord and Savior, we opted for a radical obedience to Scripture as our departure point for the development of our identity. This meant reading the Bible from the perspective of those who experienced poverty, imprisonment and oppression. We rejected the West's accumulated and assumed wealth as a starting point for our identity. We also rejected the white South African idea of a God who saw the state as all-powerful, granting divine sanction to kill anybody who stood in its way.

Second, there was an escalating repression of the black community by government forces and a growing resolve to resist that repression. As a result, violence increased. Black resistance was met with brutal military and police action which found support from a significant number of white Evangelicals. At the same time the police action was condemned by the vast majority of blacks—including black Evangelicals. The hard question that arose was: How was it possible for people who called themselves Christians to hold opposing views on who was right on the issue of justice in South Africa?

This question inevitably resulted in the third crisis, a crisis in mission. How could black Christians preach to or have fellowship with whites when there were such inconsistencies? If God is on the side of the poor, if Christ lived and died among the poor and "had nowhere to lay his head," how could Christians preach with any authority about God and Christ while at the same time ignoring the plight of the poor and oppressed? This led to a paralysis in mission that would last for years.

In 1986 CE published a document entitled "Evangelical Witness in South Africa." The publication was prompted by an event that happened during a state of emergency that lasted from July 1985 to March 1986.

Concerned Evangelicals had been meeting and discussing various topics on a regular basis, but we had no plans of making a public declaration of our discussions. We simply wanted to inform ourselves so that we could act responsibly in our individual ministries. The incident that finally forced us to speak out came in late 1985.

Curfews were being enforced in some areas and the security forces were invading schools and arresting even eight-year-olds. While we were meeting in one of the churches in Orlando, Soweto, the security forces stormed into the school next to the church. In order to avoid capture, kids were smashing window panes and jumping through the broken glass to escape. The same security forces then attacked a second school some 200 meters from the church. Our group felt helpless and could do nothing to stop these brutal acts.

Then a violent counter-attack followed. The students became so angry about what the security forces did to them that they took to the streets and went on a rampage. They stoned a number of commercial vehicles that passed by, and they managed to set one on fire after letting the driver go.

As this new violence unfolded before us we agonized about our role in this situation. If we failed to intervene in the legalized brutal violence of the security forces, what right did we have to intervene in the counter-violence of the students? What was our response supposed to be as black evangelical Christians in this situation? This would not be the last such incident and we knew it. We needed to respond.

From this point on, each time we met we asked one of our group to prepare a short paper on a topic specifically related to our society's current conditions, offering a fresh evangelical perspective. These papers were then collated and edited for publication to the wider community in South Africa. Rev. Frans Kekana, Frank Chikane and I were asked to edit the papers.

The editing of what would become "Evangelical Witness in South Africa" was made difficult by the fact that Frank Chikane had gone underground. He took enormous risks each time he came out of hiding to go over any changes that needed to be made. This meant that we had to time our rendezvous carefully: one slip and I would miss him or jeopardize his whereabouts or, worse, get both of us picked up by the security police. Today we look back on our clandestine activities and laugh. Then, it was serious business.

The final paragraph of "Evangelical Witness in South Africa" summed up our thinking.

> *We call upon all committed Evangelicals*
> *in South Africa to come out boldly to be*
> *witnesses of the gospel of salvation,*
> *justice and peace in this country without*
> *fear. You have not received the spirit of*
> *slavery to fall back into fear (Romans*
> *8:15) as many of us have done. We have*
> *to take a stand now even if it may mean*
> *persecution by earthly systems. For if we*
> *fail now we shall have no legitimacy in*
> *the post-liberation period unless we want*
> *to join the hypocrites of this world.*

Through the encouragement of the Institute for Contextual Theology we were able to print and distribute 1,500 copies of our book.

What began as a fellowship of seven men in 1985 has grown today into a national movement that has organized an accredited Evangelical Theological House of Studies at the University of Natal, on the Pietermaritzburg campus. Eleven students are presently studying there for theological degrees. In addition, CE regularly holds campaigns and seminars on wide-ranging issues related to Third World/ First World problems in South Africa, as well as seminars on evangelism and lectures on strategies to empower the poor and oppressed to become whole persons in all areas of life.

Two more voices from completely different viewpoints were added to the chorus of pain in South Africa. The first was Rev. Michael Cassidy's book *The Passing Summer*. Although written from the perspective of a white South African Evangelical who saw the "passing summer" of white privilege as a threat to the peace and stability of the region, it nevertheless sounded a clear warning: catastrophe lurked around the corner for this country unless white people truly repented and blacks responded with forgiveness.

A second book, *God in South Africa* by Father Albert Nolan, portrays a South Africa where the "Christian life cannot be interpreted correctly unless it is done from within the community of the oppressed." While both men wrote from different perspectives on the crisis in South Africa, it is clear that they both recognized the critical stage to which South Africa had come by the end of 1988.

My involvement as CE chairman helped me to raise the issues that had to be dealt with by the church if a prophetic voice was going to be heard. The more I challenged the church to take the political situation seriously, the more I realized we were not prepared to deal with specific issues relating to the solutions we advocated.

It wasn't enough to say that the church must advocate land redistribution, we also had to contribute meaningful advice as to how this might be achieved. A further question had to be asked: Are there biblical principles that could be applied to these vexing questions? If so, what were they and how could we state them in such a way as to get a hearing with the rest of society, including political leaders?

A new organization calling itself the Jubilee Initiative offered me a forum to apply scriptural values to society. Jubilee Initiative was set up to explore biblically based alternatives for managing a new South Africa. This was precisely what I was looking for.

I got involved in this think tank at the invitation of Dr. Michael Schluter of the Jubilee Centre in Cambridge, England. A number of us had been invited as a result of his desire to do something for the South African situation. He had been involved with the World Bank in Kenya for many years and had done significant research enabling the bank to make policy decisions about investments in the rural areas of East Africa.

138

It was argued by the Jubilee Initiative that because the majority of South Africans said they were Christians, or at least asserted Christian values, it was possible to seize the "middle ground"—people who realized that what bound them together was stronger than what divided them.

The Jubilee Initiative commissioned research on a wide range of topics including land reform, urbanization and housing, business (ownership and structures), education, welfare, defense and security.

In time the Initiative became uniquely South African by cutting all links with England. But before this happened a scandalous article appeared in the *New Nation,* a weekly newspaper considered by blacks to be the mouthpiece of progressive organizations within the Mass Democratic Movement. The article alleged that Jubilee Initiative was a foreign concept with no mandate from the grass roots within the country. In short, it was portrayed as another neocolonial attempt by British conservatives to manipulate "peace-loving church leaders" to circumvent the liberation movement's attempts to end apartheid.

The article was so vicious that it had the potential of destroying the credibility I had within the Mass Democratic Movement. It would also, because of my leadership in them, make my ministry with Youth Alive, Ebenezer Evangelical Church and Concerned Evangelicals very suspect. I had to clear this erroneous image of myself and the distortions of Jubilee Initiative as well. This was to prove very difficult.

I was in the United States when the article appeared in Johannesburg. Chumi called to tell me about the article and the negative effects it was having in the community. I had to respond immediately. I wrote a rebuttal and faxed it directly to the *New Nation.* My response to the article was published immediately, but the effect of my letter was not nearly as powerful as the original article. When I returned to South Africa I went on the offensive, phoning leaders like Zwelakhe Sisulu who was the newspaper's editor—a man of integrity and wisdom whose control was often wrested from him by the government. He was very sympathetic to the problem and wrote an additional article allowing me to present my point of view.

While this was going on, my brothers and sisters within CE asked me to resign from Jubilee Initiative because they felt my continued involvement would compromise them. I asked them to reconsider, both because of the concerns I had for Jubilee itself and because of the negative effect my resignation would have on fellow members of the Initiative.

As difficult as it was to hold on to Jubilee, I'm glad that I did. Now we are negotiating with several key organizations like the South African Catholic Bishops conference, the Institute for Contextual Theology and the South African Council of Churches, all of whom see the need for an evangelical contribution in the political debate. The endorsement by these organizations has enabled Jubilee to have a more far-reaching influence than we could have anticipated before the mean-spirited article was printed. Everything ultimately turned out for our good.

18

Youth Alive and Ebenezer
Evangelical Church

I was converted in 1967 through the ministry of Youth Alive.
It was a time when many African theologians and politicians
were calling for a moratorium on missionary work in Africa.
The rise of African nationalism was eradicating anything that
smacked of cultural imperialism and the colonial era. For
Youth Alive, that "colonial era" had existed, in one form or
another, since the 1800s.

In the nineteenth century, the British-led South Africa
General Mission appeared in Cape Town to evangelize and
start churches among the African people. As the mission
grew and expanded north, the British were joined by American and Australian missionaries, and the name was changed
to Africa Evangelical Fellowship to reflect the organization's
international nature.

It was from this organization that an American missionary
couple, Mr. and Mrs. Allen Lutz, emerged to found Youth
Alive in 1960. They began their mission work with an African
couple, Mr. and Mrs. Jerry Nkosi, in the teeming sprawl of
Soweto. At the same time, the AEF founded the Africa
Evangelical church in Soweto, of which I was later a
member. The AEF saw itself as the parent organization for
the work of Youth Alive, and it actively supported the Lutz
family while continuing to develop its own ministry.

There was tremendous anticipation and hope in the early
days. The first few years saw blacks and missionaries working

well together. In time, however, the relationship between AEF and Youth Alive began to deteriorate as more and more black leaders emerged in the organization.

The missionaries felt that they were losing control. This was aggravated by Allen Lutz's goal to have Youth Alive totally independent of AEF, and himself out of the organization within ten years. By 1976 he had exceeded his ten-year goal and he wanted to relinquish his responsibilities. He was opposed to a continued missionary presence in the organization and felt it was time to leave. The AEF, however, did not approve of his departure; the notion of black leadership was unthinkable. They held on to the old-fashioned, racist view that black people could not run organizations by themselves.

Despite the parent organization's disparaging view of black South Africans, Youth Alive was my spiritual home at this time. The leaders taught me that Jesus is Lord of all areas of life and that everybody is somebody. They nourished my spiritual roots and helped me to shape my response to the South African dilemma. With the Lutzes' departure from Youth Alive in 1976, our ties with outside organizations were severed, and I was asked to become the new executive director.

My first task as Youth Alive's first full-time director following the 1976 riots was to establish a new organizational structure. The changes I planned were deeply influenced by the deaths of thousands of young people during the riots between June and November of 1976, and by the thousands of students who fled into exile to join liberation movements. At the same time, YA found itself part of the black religious community that now challenged the church to respond to the tremendous human suffering all around us and the structures that perpetrated this suffering.

We changed the organization's name to Youth Alive Ministries to more accurately reflect our emphasis on ministry; YAM would now respond in a more holistic way to the full range of our young people's needs. We maintained a strong community-development program and promoted

142

public debate on social-justice issues while proclaiming the gospel and evangelizing young people. A new constitution was adopted that adhered to the democratic principles which later became the battle cry of many other community organizations. On the strength of this constitution, YAM was enabled to grow beyond the boundaries of Soweto, expanding into other regions such as Cape Town, Zululand, Zimbabwe and Swaziland.

One of the challenges that our leaders faced as we matured in our understanding of social-justice issues was to clarify those issues for the expatriate missionary community. They had been supportive of YAM, but they were now wavering because of our emphasis on a God who demands justice both from individuals and governments.

Understanding the entire black struggle was difficult for white missionaries. On the one hand they felt that politics and talk of political change were not part of the gospel mandate; the salvation of souls was the all-important thing. It was a simple dichotomy in their minds. On the other hand, as whites they did not live among the Africans to whom they were called to minister and preach the gospel; they could not know the real suffering and hardship we faced every day of our lives. They could not, or would not, see the evil of apartheid and how we were treated as a race of second-class citizens. They retreated at night to their all-white suburban homes and their black maids, oblivious to our pain.

The missionaries' limited knowledge of the black community was far superior to that of the white South Africans who feared and despised blacks. However, it was still very hard for missionaries to understand the transformation black youth had undergone as a result of the 1976 uprisings. They could not reconcile the happy, clapping, chorus-singing young people who came to their Sunday-school meetings with the angry, white-hating, bitter black youths who now demanded that missionaries leave their high-school campuses.

The 1976 uprisings created an even bigger gulf between us and the foreign missionary establishment. Most of the

143

missionaries had stopped coming into Soweto at the outbreak of the riots. They were afraid for their lives. Some of them justified their actions by claiming that their black brothers and sisters would be considered "Uncle Toms" or sell-outs for their continued fraternizing with the "enemy of the people." Since they did not want to compromise their brethren, they would "sacrificially" stay away. As a result, a lot of those missionaries completely lost touch with the realities of black aspirations. (While the evangelical missionaries fled Soweto, Catholic and Episcopal nuns and priests continued to live in the townships despite repeated threats to their lives. This gave credibility to the witness of these two large denominations.) Youth Alive Ministries had to deal with these realities when presenting the gospel to the youth who came to us with questions about the injustices that had been done to them and their families. We could not dodge these issues; they had to be faced head-on.

Opposition to the new YAM approach to ministry came not only from the foreign missionaries but from a number of black evangelical pastors as well. These pastors too, had accepted the old dichotomy between the spiritual and the sociopolitical demands of the gospel. While they may have hated apartheid, they would say nothing against it; such statements might be interpreted as political, and pastors were opposed to any mixing of politics with religion. It was as though the 1976 riots had never occurred.

Some of these pastors opposed us because they were afraid of offending the white people upon whom they depended for their support. I was deeply saddened when I heard black pastors say that even if you did not agree with these white "superiors," you did not have to tell them: they might withhold their financial support and you might go hungry.

Many of us went hungry in those early days. We paid a price for our faith and we would not compromise the gospel just to fill our bellies. To be silent on either account would be a betrayal of what we knew as true. Furthermore, we were seeing young people coming to faith in Christ, and to change our strategy and emphases now would have been a betrayal of our mission to minister to all aspects of these young people's lives. We had faith that in due time the broader evangelical world in South Africa and the West would come to realize and accept this. I believed then, as I do now, that if we had changed our message during a crisis, we would have no message at all when the crisis was over.

Youth Alive had no desire to see young Christian converts divorce their new-found faith from personal lives often marked by unemployment, harassment, humiliation and despair. Nor could we allow them to gloss over or forget the apartheid that kept them enslaved. We wanted them to join churches that were living out the gospel of faith and repentance while being sensitive to the evil of apartheid.

As difficult as it was for missionaries in South Africa to understand what we were doing, it was going to prove much more difficult for people in the United States and Europe. Many of these Christians branded us "Communists" because they believed our opposition to the state was unbiblical and because they believed the lies propagated by the South African government. Some in these countries distanced themselves from us.

This was personally painful for me. I had studied in the West and spoken in hundreds of churches about our ministry and what it was trying to accomplish. The misunderstanding of our situation deepened my anguish, but it also strengthened my resolve not to cave in. I thank God we were never tempted to water down our stance or abandon evangelism and the call to social justice.

The essential difference between YAM and the black churches that had been founded by missionaries was the issue of control. YAM could act independently. These churches could not. They depended on the missionary establishment for their financial support and, therefore, had to toe the party line. We didn't. The only drawback was that our independence meant we had to work all the harder to make ends meet financially.

I had previously developed many potential supporters for the ministry of YAM while speaking in North American churches. In these churches were men and women who agreed to pray for us and who also wanted to support us financially. What we desired now was an organization in the States that would channel financial support to YAM in Soweto.

To my mind African Evangelical Fellowship was the natural place to start. AEF did not agree. After several meetings with the general secretary, my request to have AEF funds directed to us was turned down. I was shocked.

I discovered that old ways remained entrenched even in the face of changing times. I was told that my lack of "foreign-ness" in South Africa disqualified me as a missionary. I therefore could not be funded in my particular mission—Youth Alive. I was also told that I could not participate in the same form of fund raising that foreign missionaries used. Furthermore, I could not participate in missionary structures because I was a "national" and my needs were different from those of white missionaries. AEF's rejection was an affront to me and the clear call I had been given by God to minister and serve in Youth Alive Ministries—a call that had been affirmed by AEF's own board. But the decision was final.

As I reflected on their decision over the following weeks and months, I also began to study missionary organizations and their strategies on the mission field. The more I studied, the more I saw that the structures they erected actually encouraged the subservience of black nationals to white missionaries.

Western missionaries were never accountable to the local church on the mission field. Instead their activities were determined by a field council made up of other missionaries, completely without black African participation. Blacks were neither invited nor wanted in the decision-making process. Tragically, decisions made by Western missionaries controlled the destiny of the black church.

A missionary whom I confronted in the States about the paternalism of his mission said, "I have worked with Africans for thirty years and I know what they need." What he meant was that Africans needed continued missionary care because they would never be mature enough to make their own decisions.

The problem was compounded by the fact that there was no fellowship among missionary-birthed churches within the black community. All the relationships went from the black community church upward to the missionary council at the top. This meant that black Evangelicals never reflected on their problems together within their context or environment. This unhappy situation persists to this day.

I realized that the black evangelical community would have to be free of outmoded structures and outdated mission practices if we were to be effective witnesses in a changing South Africa. I saw the need for a church where I could work with my black brothers and sisters in a way that would speak to their bodies and souls, but never one to the exclusion of the other. I sought a balanced approach to evangelism in Soweto, where the battle was being fought for the hearts and minds of young people.

Previously I had been a lay leader in the Africa Evangelical Church, working under the direction of the Rev. Sipho Bhengu, the pastor. Even though I was not a pastor, I participated in the pulpit ministry and in the counseling of young people. I grew to love this church and it helped to shape my desire to be in full-time ministry. I was convinced that the local church should play a critical role in God's overall redemptive purposes in history. My deepest longing was to play a part in that redemptive history.

Before leaving South Africa in 1970 to study in the United States, I was asked to become the Rev. Bhengu's assistant. I accepted. During my year with him, I grew in my faith and knowledge of Jesus Christ and sharpened my preaching and counseling skills. The church grew, and I knew that, whatever lay in store for me in the States, I would return here.

During the years I was away, I frequently corresponded with the Rev. Bhengu, and his letters encouraged me in my studies. What was not coming through in our correspondence, however, were the growing differences in our thinking about the political situation of South Africa.

I had become far more progressive in my attitude toward political involvement. I no longer passively accepted the traditional black role in South Africa. I felt that the church should be a prophetic voice speaking to political organizations whether they be government or anti-government, local or national.

Five years later, when I returned and rejoined this congregation, I was uncomfortable with our local church's stance. By 1979 it became clear to me that my time as part of this church was over. I resigned my position as assistant pastor and left the congregation. The whole episode left me feeling depressed. When a church is split apart or members feel compelled to leave, the powers of darkness have won another victory.

I thought of joining a neighboring AEC congregation, encouraged by Joshua Malefaka "Faki" Bodibe, a close friend who was already a member there. Faki would become a tireless coworker with me over the next three years and would prove to be one of the wisest persons to minister alongside me. He had been an independent businessman before joining Youth Alive. Many times when I wanted to throw in the towel Faki would reason with me and say I should not confuse a skirmish with the war. I am grateful for this man whose easy style and manner have helped keep me on an even keel when the political and religious winds have blown around me.

While I was contemplating what I should do and where I could use my pastoral gifts, a small group of former members of Rev. Bhengu's church had begun to meet together in the living room of a home to worship and pray together. Having made the break from a church that was controlled by white missionaries, this group of struggling believers wanted to model a form of church leadership that took the gospel seriously in the context of Soweto. Their determination to structure the church around the real needs of people, and not the needs that were perceived by outsiders, was a radical departure from the past. The group began to attract more people, and as a result they were forced to move to a two-car garage for worship. They invited me to join them.

It was a hard decision for me to make. I knew that my going to this breakaway group might be interpreted as encouraging divisions among church members. I accepted the invitation on condition that we try to effect a reconciliation with the Rev. Bhengu. For the next eighteen months we pursued every avenue for reconciliation and healing. But it was to no avail. At the end of the eighteen months, we abandoned any further attempts.

Our numbers grew week by week and we were forced to move from a garage to a school classroom in Dobsonville. In July 1982 we made the final break from the old church. After several days of prayer and congregational discussion we publicly announced our intention to be constituted as Ebenezer Evangelical Church. The name "Ebenezer" means "Thus far has the Lord led us," and it seemed a fitting title for a new congregation that had grown so much in numbers and spiritual understanding during the preceding two years—despite racial and religious turmoil.

Despite our frequent struggles, we were up and running. We had carefully written a constitution that embodied our ideals of spiritual ministry and social responsibility. We were committed to multiple leadership, teaching the Bible as the authoritative Word of God, preaching the gospel message to all who would hear, and caring for one another. We wanted to maintain a balance between preaching the gospel of God's grace and speaking out on sociopolitical conditions. While this balance was not always easy to maintain, we knew we were called to announce God's message in its totality.

We remained in that school classroom for more than seven

years, during which time we grew large enough to start a sister church in Mohlakeng, a township about ten miles away. This congregation is led currently by Moss Ntlha, national coordinator for Concerned Evangelicals, and his wife, Khumo.

One of our greatest new challenges was the need for a permanent church home. Although we were happy where we were, we could not stay there indefinitely: the Department of Education and Training had issued a directive to the school boards that all school buildings could be used only for educational purposes. For some time the principal of the school had ignored the directive. But our time had come; we needed to look for other space.

In Soweto this is a complicated procedure. In order to obtain land, one had to have either high political connections or affiliation with a large Christian denomination. We had neither. It took us four long years before the local authority could be persuaded to offer us property in Dobsonville. We paid 10,000 rand (about $4,500). This wiped out our seven-year savings of tithes and offerings. We were penniless, but we had turned the corner. Over the next three years, and with a lot of ingenuity, we raised 50,000 rand ($22,000) to build the first phase of the church.

It was the congregation's desire not to have full-time paid pastors. We wanted to explore a new leadership model. We sought to have those who demonstrated the spiritual gifts described in the Bible (explored in the New Testament in Romans, chapter 12; 1 Corinthians, chapter 12; and Ephesians, chapter 4) as our models for church leadership. We wanted to move away from the old hierarchical, top-heavy model of leadership that had been passed down to us by missionaries. By not paying salaries we had more money for those in the church who were suffering personal privations. Many of our people lived in twelve-by-twelve corrugated iron shacks, and we were able to help them get beyond the subsistence level.

We began building in November 1987. Bureaucratic red

tape and endless technical difficulties delayed the completion of the building for more than a year. But in March 1990 we dedicated the first phase of the church building and we moved in. On the first Sunday in March more than 150 people walked into the new church building rejoicing together. This was a great encouragement to us. It was the realization of a long-held dream.

Epilogue

Over the years Chumi and I have expressed our thoughts on partnership with those at Ebenezer and with friends overseas. We strongly believe that true partnership must be characterized by mutuality, accountability and availability. A number of overseas churches shared our desire to realize these ideals with Ebenezer and, where possible, with Youth Alive Ministries.

One church in Germany and another in the United States have entered into partnership with us. These partnerships have opened up possibilities for us to engage in reciprocal missions. We have begun to share our gifts and abilities. Old ways of relating, old barriers, have come tumbling down.

I salute my brothers and sisters in the Heckinghausen Congregation in Wuppertal, West Germany, who struggle to be a living community among mainline churches and endeavor to be a credible connection between evangelism and social ministry. They have supported us and encouraged others within Germany to become partners with us.

I also salute my brothers and sisters of Cornerstone Christian Fellowship in West Chester, Pennsylvania, who have over the past two years grappled with issues of evangelism and social justice both locally and nationally. They sacrificially sent Cliff and Eileen Buckwalter and their two children, Ben and Leah, to work with us in Soweto. We remember fondly the year's sabbatical leave we spent in West Chester, getting to know our brothers and sisters, and forming relationships that have been sustained over time and distance.

Like Ebenezer Church, Youth Alive Ministries has also grown and expanded. Four of the five regions where YAM is active—Cape Town, Soweto, Zululand and Zimbabwe—have regional directors. Together they now minister to more than 3,500 young men and women on a weekly basis.

The ministries range from evangelizing on high-school campuses to helping homeless kids reunite with their families and rejoin the educational system. YAM has begun food programs, including a daily soup kitchen, in two of the worst areas in Soweto. Vegetables are distributed to destitute families, and cottage industries have been started to provide poor families with a small income. Nutritional guidance and hygiene programs have also been initiated among women and children.

The major part of the YAM program, however, is made up of club activities. It is here that high-school-age Christians gather together into groups of up to 100 to work and grow. This was my personal route to faith.

In these club activities young people develop leadership skills by being given responsibility for administration as well as minor pastoral work. Many of these young people are called on to talk about their faith in Jesus Christ under difficult circumstances, and many come through with flying colors.

One of the guiding principles of this club-style ministry is maximum participation by young people during club meetings. It is here that leadership qualities are discovered, developed and deployed. The concept of training and then entrusting young people to lead raises the level of expectation. Creative forces are unleashed.

The social aspect of our work has always been motivated by the challenge to faithfully follow Jesus Christ in all situations of life. With this holistic approach, the potential of Youth Alive-type ministries in South Africa is limitless.

We are growing and prospering. We are seeing and experiencing healing in the lives of thousands of young people. God is greatly enlarging his kingdom through our ministry.

I am now forty years old. I have emerged from the bitterness of my early youth, the loss of a leg, and my hatred of whites into that glorious freedom that is mine as a child of God.

The struggle to remain faithful to God continues, but my trust in him who is Lord of all is still my sure foundation. As long as I live, I want nothing more than to see the church of Jesus Christ in South Africa rise triumphantly from the ashes of colonialism and the bankruptcy of apartheid to proclaim the living Lord who saves people from their sins and from the shackles of poverty, injustice and racism. The struggle will be long and hard.

I often describe the situation in South Africa as being five minutes past midnight. It is still night, but a faint glow appears on the horizon that brings the fresh hope of a new day. We have inched past the darkest time of our oppression under apartheid. There is the promise of a new day and new opportunities for all.

The clock cannot be turned back. Events in the political arena have reached the point of no return. The voices of the oppressed have been heard around the world. They will not be stilled till all are free.

Glossary

Africa Evangelical Fellowship

A white-run missionary organization that was started at the turn of the century in South Africa to evangelize black South Africans.

African National Congress

A political organization founded in 1912 to oppose apartheid. Banned in 1961, the movement then accepted the armed struggle as a legitimate means to overthrow the present government. The ban was removed in 1990.

Afrikaans

The official language of South Africa, having developed from seventeenth-century Dutch.

Afrikaner

White Dutch descendants who have occupied the Cape of Africa since 1652.

Apartheid

Literally "separateness" or "apartness," this is the official policy of strict racial segregation as practiced in South Africa.

Baas

A term of deference whites expect blacks to use when addressing them.

Bantu

The official name that the Nationalist Party government gave to all blacks in 1948. Prime Minister Hendrik Verwoerd wanted the use of the word "African" to apply only to Afrikaners. The political use of this word is rejected by blacks, who see it as a symbol of political disinheritance.

Broederbond

A secretive underground political force committed to sustaining the white ruling power of South Africa.

Caspirs

Mine-proof military vehicles which can be driven on any terrain. They have a terrifying effect on those whom they are attacking.

Funerals

During the period after the riots in 1976, the funerals of political activists became major platforms for political education of the Black masses. The government sought to curb this use of funerals by means of various emergency regulations.

Gideons

An international organization of Christian businessmen whose primary mission is to place Bibles in public buildings, such as hotels. In South Africa the Gideons also distribute Bibles in schools.

Homelands

Eight townships set aside by the government as the sanctioned residential areas for blacks, where a measure of self-government is allowed.

Kaffir

A term derived from Islam to define an infidel. It is a derogatory word used by whites when addressing blacks in South Africa. *Kaffir Boy* by Mark Mathabane exposes the dehumanizing effects of this word. In the context of the United States, "kaffir" is the equivalent of "nigger."

Khoisan

The first tribes encountered by the Dutch when they settled in the Cape peninsula.

Kruger, Paul

Became the first president of the South African Republic in 1883.

Mass Democratic Movement

A loose coalition of progressive organizations committed to a nonracial South Africa, who believe that you cannot oppose apartheid while participating in government structures.

Reef

A geographical stretch of land, 175-miles long, along which gold-mining towns, including Johannesburg, sprung up to mine the rich deposits.

Sharpville

The black township where the 1960 massacre occurred. Police opened fire on an unarmed crowd at the close of a peaceful protest march organized by the ANC and PAC against the "pass laws". There had been no order for the people to disperse. In the end, 69 people were lying dead and 178 wounded. 155 people were shot from behind. Those injured included 40 women and 8 children.

Soweto
A township fifteen miles southwest of Johannesburg. Its primary purpose was to provide accommodation for black laborers employed by white businesses in Johannesburg. Residence in this area was not originally intended to be permanent.

Soweto Committee of Ten
An organization which was established under the chairpersonship of Dr. N. Moblana in 1978. The organization developed black civic associations who embarked on campaigns to discredit the government-sponsored local municipalities called urban councils.

Verwoerd, Hendrik
The first Minister of Bantu Education. He later became prime minister. He is the architect of apartheid and developed the model of Bantu Homelands in 1936.

Volk
An Afrikaan word which literally means "folk", but which has become synonymous with the Afrikaner's self-understanding of being pure and having a special mission for God in the world.

Voortrekkers
Bands of Dutch settlers who moved to the north from the Cape colony to escape British rule.

White spot
Used to denote a formerly black-occupied land which, in the process of the consolidation of the homelands, would be expropriated and given to whites.

Recommended Reading

Aeschliman, Gordon D. *Apartheid: Tragedy in Black and White*. Ventura, California: Regal Books, 1986.

Cassidy, Michael. *The Passing Summer: A South African Pilgrimage in the Politics of Love*. London: Hodder & Stoughton, 1989. California: Regal Books, 1990.

Concerned Evangelicals. *Evangelical Witness in South Africa*. Grand Rapids, Michigan: Wm. B. Eerdmans, 1986.

Lodge, Tom. *Black Politics in South Africa*. Athens, Ohio: Ohio University Press, 1986.

Lodge, Tom. *Resistance Ideology in Settler Societies*. Athens, Ohio: Ohio University Press, 1986.

Lodge, Tom. *The Creation of a Mass Movement: Strikes and Defiance 1950–1952*. Johannesburg: University of Witwatersrand, 1981.

Meer, Fatima. *Nelson Mandela*. London: Penguin Books, 1988.

Nolan, Albert. *God in South Africa: The Challenge of the Gospel*. Grand Rapids, Michigan: Wm. B. Eerdmans, 1988.

Pascoe, Elaine. *South Africa: Troubled Land*. New York: Franklin Watts, 1987.

Paton, Alan. *Cry the Beloved Country*. London: Jonathan Cape, 1948.

Ryan, Colleen. *Beyers Naude, Pilgrimage of Faith*. Grand Rapids, Michigan: Wm. B. Eerdmans, 1990.

South Africa in the 1980's: State of Emergency. London: Catholic Institute for International Relations, 1980.

Sparks, Allister. *The Mind of South Africa*. New York: Knopf, 1990.

Wink, Walter. *Violence and Nonviolence in South Africa*. Philadelphia, Pennsylvania: New Society Publishers, 1987.